First published by
The Social Market Foundation,
December 2004

The Social Market Foundation
11 Tufton Street
London SW1P 3QB

Designed by Paula Snell Design

Contents

Introduction **4**

Choice in theory **6**

Analysing the evidence **15**

School choice: summary of findings **19**

School choice: UK **23**

School choice: US **39**

School choice: New Zealand **56**

School choice: Chile **62**

School choice: Sweden **68**

School choice: Conclusions **73**

Patient choice: Summary of findings **82**

Patient choice: UK **85**

Patient choice: international **99**

Patient choice: conclusions **107**

General policy implications **111**

School choice: what are the policy implications? **114**

Patient choice: what are the policy implications? **119**

SMF programme of work on choice and voice **124**

Introduction

To date, there has been no systematic review of the international and domestic research on the impact of extending user choice in public services. This publication is an attempt to provide that review and to move the debate about the impact of new choice schemes in the UK from a theoretical analysis to an evidence-based one.

There is serious disagreement over the extension of choice in public services. A whole range of views has now been expressed as to the way in which choice might affect quality, efficiency and equity in public services. Some commentators see trade-offs within these three: others are either pessimistic or optimistic on all counts.

The paper aims to inject some clarity into this debate. It is the product of extensive research by the Social Market Foundation into the national and international evidence on the employment and impact in practice of choice-based schemes in the public services. While we do discuss the theoretical arguments in favour of and against the extension of choice in the UK, our main aim is to determine from the evidence what effect choice schemes have in terms of equity and efficiency. We are assuming that both the design of choice schemes and the context in which they are introduced will make a difference to these outcomes. For this reason we have attempted consistently to relate outcomes to the basic design of choice policies, as well as to the wider context in which they are introduced. We believe that this should ensure that the results will be of use to the debate on choice as it applies to the UK. We have limited our scope to schemes in the health and education sectors. This is where the majority of literature is focused and, together with local government, it is the main focus of political debate in the UK.

1 Note: Some readers may be surprised that neither Denmark nor the Netherlands is included in our review of the evidence on school choice. These countries certainly offer radical and unique models of school choice; however we have found very little evidence that goes beyond describing the way in which they are designed, and for this reason we have excluded them.

Choice policies invite an enormous range of values and concerns and we could not realistically cover them all. Instead we have identified practical questions that we believe cover some of the most substantive issues, based on the major concerns that are raised about the introduction of choice mechanisms into public services in the UK. These have their variations (see the next chapter); however the four most basic questions are:

1. where recipients have been offered choice, have they taken it up?

2. where recipients have taken up choice, *which* recipients have done so?

3. what has been the effect of choice on the quality and efficiency of providers; in particular, what has been the effect on those service users that have *not* exercised choice?

4. for education specifically, what has been the effect of parental choice on segregation in public education?

We have asked these questions of all countries where there has been substantive evidence on these issues, although in general we have prioritised results from the UK. This has meant looking in particular at the UK, the US, the Netherlands, Denmark, Norway, Sweden, Chile and New Zealand. In each case we have tried to relate outcomes as closely as possible to the basic design of each policy. We have paid attention to a range of variables including: the arrangements governing funding; the nature of the supply side; the freedoms available to professionals in responding to recipients' choices; the arrangements for supporting recipients in making them; and finally the context in which choice has operated, in particular for urban and non-urban areas. We hope that, in doing so, we will have produced a document that can inform the debate on choice taking places within the UK[1].

In our conclusion, we draw out what we believe to be the main lessons from this review of the evidence for those considering the introduction of further choice mechanisms into UK public services, and set out our on-going programme of work on these issues.

Choice in theory

Taxonomy of choice

When politicians and policymakers talk about introducing
or extending choice in public services, it is often unclear
which of a range of models or system designs they are referring
to. For the purposes of this paper, will be use the following
taxonomy:

(a) when we talk about **choice** systems in this paper, we
     are referring to systems in which individual service users
     are offered a choice between different providers of a public
     service. This generates contestability between providers.
     This does not imply that the choice on offer is between
     public and private sector providers – it may equally be
     between two different public sector providers (for example
     between two hospitals). This type of individual choice
     may also be deferred to an agent.

(b) a second way in which choice may be offered is
     through **collective choice**, in which service users are
     asked, as a group, to make decisions about the kind of
     service they want.

(c) a variant of option (b) is when **collective choice** is
     conducted by proxy. An agent or representative of service
     users will make choices based on the needs or wishes
     of service users. An example of this is the way in which
     Primary Care Trusts (PCTs) buy services on behalf
     of users.

(d) when we refer instead to individual service users being
     offered a choice of services from a single provider,
     we will refer to this as **choice of services**.

In this paper, we will be looking at (a), the individual choice of provider model. For the sake of brevity, we will refer to this as choice.

There are two related concepts which are often brought into the discussion about choice: personalisation and voice. Definitions of both these concepts are contested, but loosely speaking, personalisation can be said to be the attempt to match public services more closely to the needs of the user. This might be achieved through any number of mechanisms, including choice mechanisms. Voice, again loosely conceived, might be said to be the direct representation of user views to those running a public service.

These two concepts are not the subject of this review of the evidence and so are only lightly touched on here, although we return to them when setting out the next phase of the Social Market Foundation's research in this area.

User involvement and contestability

Underpinning the choice definitions set out above are two sets of ideas for public services, both of which enjoy a considerable amount of political currency and both of which have the aim of improving the quality of public services through better meeting the needs of service users. On the one hand there are a number of ideas that fall under the general heading of 'user involvement'. These vary, but the common aim is to encourage services to engage more closely with the different needs and preferences of their individual recipients or their constituency. Second there is a set of ideas that fall under the heading of 'contestability'. These are financial mechanisms the aim of which is to motivate providers to deliver services which meet the needs of their users, through the threat that their funding could go to an alternative provider.

The choice of provider model

The theory underpinning the choice of provider model suggests that it *necessarily* involves certain characteristics if it is to deliver the benefits promised for it. In particular, it will need to have, at least to some extent, the following sets of characteristics:

1. the public service provider in question has some degree of management control over finances and other aspects of service delivery

If a choice scheme is to have the effects promised for it then it must be sufficiently *demand sensitive*. One of the most obvious and oft-noted requirements is that demand should be able to expand with supply. However, if we are to expect public services to respond substantively to recipients' choices and preferences, then those services must have sufficient flexibility to respond and to bring about desired improvements. Most importantly, this implies some flexibility in the use of *inputs*, in particularly *some budgetary* flexibility. This degree of financial autonomy does not imply that public services should be subject to less assessment, or that they should be able to choose the services they provide or the individuals to whom they provide them, or even that they should be exempt from centrally determined targets and priorities.

2 On the other hand, while choice implies some form of flexibility and payment by results, flexibility and payment by results do not necessarily imply choice. In a recent paper for the SMF Gordon Brown advocates flexibility and payment by results for the NHS, while expressing some doubts about the benefits of increased choice. Brown, G A *Modern Agenda for Prosperity and Social Reform: Opportunity, Security, Prosperity*, Social Market Foundation.

2.   **a proportion of public services' funding will be by results, or per recipient**
For example, this is contrasted with a system in which services are funded on the basis of the previous year's activity. Arrangements can be more or less ambitious in tailoring funding to circumstances, but the basic principle is that funding only arrives with a service when the recipient does. This is important since it ensures that there are substantive consequences for the service provider attracting and for losing recipients. By itself, this principle can apply at a number of administrative levels – the individual service, groups of services, the municipality, and so on.

A choice-based model which does not have these features is unlikely to produce productive efficiency gains[2]. These criteria provide a useful benchmark by which to evaluate the schemes discussed below, and any proposed schemes in the UK. Introducing choice, flexibility and payment by results into a public service generates additional costs as well as additional benefits, and a critical question to ask of any proposal to extend choice on this model is whether the benefits outweigh additional costs.

Advocates of this model claim the following benefits:

- services will become more tailored to individual needs and differences and will engage with, and include, recipients (personalisation, user involvement, allocative efficiency)

- more basically, they will allocate supply to demand more efficiently (allocative efficiency)

- they will generate greater quality for a fixed level of funding (productive efficiency)

- benefits will accrue both to those who actually exercise choice but also to those who do not – because the exercise and threat of choice will give all providers the incentives and the information to improve (this is generally what is meant by the claim that choice has a 'levelling up effect' on the quality of public services).

Equity and the choice of provider model

In the evidence section of this paper we look at how the models of choice under consideration deviate from the theoretical model outlined above. We also have identified a number of other factors which may, in theory, have an impact on the equity of outcomes. These include:

- whether choice is limited to a specific class of recipient

- whether it applies only in specific circumstances, for example after a patient has been waiting for six months or if a student meets certain socio-economic or other criteria

- whether providers are allowed openly to select their recipients (if this is the case, providers may select service users who present a lower cost or burden on the service, which in turn is likely to discriminate against the disadvantaged)

- whether recipients are supported in exercising choices, for example through transport, information and advice (if this is not the case, then the more informed and articulate may be able to monopolise new choices)

- whether recipients have the option to make choice in conjunction with a qualified agent such as a GP (again, for the reasons identified above)

- whether services are compensated for the different costs imposed by recipients (without such compensation, service providers will have an incentive to recruit service users who present a lesser cost or other burden on a provider. Whether they respond to this incentive will depend on other features, including the design of the scheme).

In our description and discussion of choice schemes in operation, where possible we have set out which of these factors each policy involves.

Objections to choice schemes
The political arguments for and against the further introduction of choice schemes have been widely rehearsed elsewhere, so we do not intend to devote a great deal of space to them here. However, these do provide a benchmark against which the evidence discussed below can be evaluated so we provide a short outline of the main arguments here.

It is worth noting that some of these objections are not conceptually distinct; nor is it always clear what assumptions are being made by those putting forward these views.

Objection A:
There is no need to introduce choice to improve the quality of public services. This can be achieved through greater investment [3].
This objection may assume that promised efficiency gains will not materialise, so that direct funding will be more effective, pound for pound and/or that choice mechanisms will generate inequalities in the provision of services.

These claims can be tested against the evidence below. It is also worth considering how effective additional funding, without reform, has been to date in delivering benefits equitably. Looking at the impact of NHS funding, it is clear that, despite considerable investment in the National Health Service since its inception, the system is characterised by profound and growing inequity in health outcomes which, whilst mainly the product of wider socio-economic trends, cannot be completely separated from the inequities fostered by the structural character of the NHS.

Objection B:
Capacity in public services is too limited to produce efficiency gains [4] while the alternative, maintaining excess capacity, is a waste of public resources.
There is a substantive concern at work here. Limited capacity does limit contestability as, for example, in school choice where

3 *For all this feverish ideological debate, there is only one way to improve schools* Johann Hari column, The Independent, 7 July 2004

4 This concern is raised in *What is the real cost of more Patient Choice* John Appleby, Anthony Harrison, Nancy Devlin, Kings Fund 2003

5 *Agitators will inherit the earth* Roy Hattersley column, The Guardian, 17 November 2003

capacity in the system is tightly restricted by design. There are three possible responses to this concern which should be subject to a review of the evidence:

- choice within a system with limited capacity could be expected to produce allocative efficiency gains. In other words, even choice within a system of limited capacity should be more effective at representing the wishes of individual service users than a system with no choice

- efficiency gains would outweigh the extra costs of providing excess capacity – any proposal should be subject to a cost-benefit analysis

- public services as they stand may have enough capacity for choice to be effective.

Objection C:
A lack of capacity in the system allows good providers to cherry pick the service users that they wish to take, covertly or otherwise.

Again, this point, closely related to Objection B, is a substantive concern which is borne out by the evidence of the operation of school choice in the UK. The consequences of allowing providers to select service users is that inequity in the system is likely to be exacerbated. This concern can be addressed if:

- this can be prevented by introducing excess capacity into the system, and if efficiency gains outweigh the extra costs of providing that excess capacity

- if this can be prevented not by introducing new capacity in the form of new public services, but instead by allowing increased flexibility into the system in the form of allowing the growth of good providers.

In looking at what the evidence says about this, it is worth bearing in mind that the introduction of effective voice mechanisms alongside choice mechanisms should limit movement of users between providers.

Objection D:
Choice schemes will result in unequal outcomes[5].

This objection is similar to, but broader than, the criticism made in Objection C. In considering this, it is important that the impact of any new choice model should be judged against the picture of equity generated by current services[6], or any realistic alternatives. In general, our public services allow the exercise of clandestine choice by the articulate or well off. For example, it is open to those with the resources to buy homes in the catchment areas of schools they regard as good. Similarly, those who are articulate and persuasive can often negotiate for themselves a preferential outcome when seeking healthcare.

The assumption in operation with this objection is that, by making choice explicit, you will further empower the wealthy and articulate to "game" the system and produce for themselves preferential outcomes.

This is open to the following arguments:

- although money follows the user in choice schemes, the service they receive is not dependent on making any payment, so the individual's financial situation is not relevant, given no significant access costs. This is not always the case at present: for example, under the current school admissions system, those who are better off can buy their way into the school of their choice through buying a home in the catchment area

- that the capacity to understand the information on offer about public services, and to take decisions, is critical, but that choice operating in the open allows service users access to information, and assistance with making decisions if required

Objection E:
People do not want to choose[7], they simply want good quality local services.

A recent MORI poll[8] found that 81% of those polled thought that Britain's public services need to start treating users and the public as customers. This suggests that, at least, there is an appetite for a more responsive service.

----

6 For example, inequalities in healthcare have risen since the NHS was founded, see *Is the NHS Equitable?: A Review of the Evidence*, Dixon et al, LSE Health and Care Discussion Paper Number 11

7 Stuart Jeffries argues this in *Hell is 57 Varieties* The Guardian, 8 March 2004

8 *Attitudes to Public Service Reform* MORI 6 July 2004 (Sample: 1,002; fieldwork: 2-4 July 2004)

Generalising about what "people" want is not a particularly helpful approach. Some individuals will want the option to choose, while others will not. A recent MORI poll[8] found that 81% of those polled thought that Britain's public services need to start treating users and the public as customers. This suggests that, at least, there is an appetite for a more responsive service.

There are a number of possible responses to this concern which are amenable to evaluation against the evidence base:

- choice schemes can increase the quality of public services people receive, thereby meeting an important requirement even of those who do not explicitly want the right to choose

- an effective choice scheme will include the right of people *not* to choose through providing an agent to choose on their behalf (for example a GP).

Objection F:
Introducing choice will result in the existence of persistently failing services.

This is closely related to the concern above about the equity of systems. The argument is that a choice system coupled with excess capacity and/or increased flexibility will result in poorly performing services being deserted by more articulate and informed service users. In turn, this will result in a significant loss of funding and morale. This is likely to impact most heavily on those least able to negotiate the system.

If choice mechanisms are working effectively, it is true that service users are likely to leave poorly performing service. The critical issue is the policy response to this. It is possible to argue that:

- effective mechanisms for managing failure are critical to choice schemes operating successfully. In fact, in order for services overall to improve, governments must be willing either to close failing services or to operate an interventionist system for turning them around. The challenge for the latter is to develop a system for managing failure that is consistent with the overall point of a competitive choice scheme.

Another issue to consider here is that choice systems, when supported by effective voice mechanisms, should limit exit in favour of early reform.

Objection G:
Choice will drive out cooperation between providers.

Introducing contestability into public services does not reduce service provision to a zero sum game. If this were the case, we would expect to see service users repeatedly changing provider in a bid to find the very highest quality service on offer. This is counterintuitive. Instead, we might expect people to be content with good, or very good service provision, rather than the very best[9].

If the introduction of choice does not make the provision of a public service a zero-sum game for providers, then we would expect sharing best practice to be as much of a win-win situation for providers as it is at present.

The critical question is whether or not:

- the degree of cooperation between service providers in a choice-based system should be no less than under other forms of provision.

9 Herbert Simon in *A Behavioural Model of Rational Choice, in Models of man: social and rational; mathematical essays on rational human behaviour in a social setting* John Wiley & Son, 1957, described this tendency when he said that people are only 'rational enough', and in fact relax their rationality when it is no longer required. He described this as the tendency to "satisfice" – that it to achieve a good enough solution, rather than the maximally beneficial one.

Analysing the evidence

Who Chooses?

As discussed above, the arguments in favour of extending choice in public services depend on a number of claims about what the impact of choice schemes will be in practice. This included the claim that people would make active choices in public services, and that outcomes will be no more inequitable than under current public services.

Given this objection, the first question we have sought to address from the evidence is:

- Where public services have offered more choice, have service users taken it up?

Advocates of choice policies also argue that the introduction of choice mechanisms means a move away from a system characterised by clandestine choice to one in which choice is operating in the open, thereby allowing all service users a greater opportunity to choose, and by implication, generating a more level playing field[10]. This raises the following question:

- Where choice in public services has been exercised, which people were able to exercise it effectively?

Who benefits?

A further claim by those in favour of choice is that such schemes can increase the quality of public services people receive, thereby meeting an important requirement even of those who do not explicitly want the right to choose. This generates the questions:

- Do choice schemes result in improved efficiency/quality?

- Do the benefits of efficiency outweigh any additional expenditure, such as that required to generate excess capacity of flexibility in the system?

10 Le Grand, J and Dixon, A. *Choice and Equity in the National Health Service*, 2004, unpublished document.

In so far as extended choice might add up to a more segregated public school community, then, that is one consideration against it

11 Though Ewan Ferlie's report as part of the national evaluation of the London Patient Choice Project gives some initial thoughts on this question.

There is a further claim implicit here, which is that choice acts to drive up standards *even for those who don't exercise it* which suggests that choice policies have a 'levelling-up' effect on the quality of public provision, rather than 'polarisation' between popular and unpopular providers. One of the most fundamental questions for choice policies is therefore:

- How have any costs and benefits been distributed across services and service users?

Clearly, this question is linked with the question of how service users under choice distribute themselves across services, not least because some individuals impose larger costs on services than others. Indeed, the objection that unpopular services will suffer under choice is often based as much on the assumption that these services will lose their best recipients as on the assumption that they will lose funding.

There is also a claim that contestability does not necessarily generate a lack of information sharing by service providers, so we must also ask:

- to what extent is cooperation retained between service providers in choice-based systems?

It is worth noting at this point that very little research has been conducted that bears even indirectly on this question[11]. Therefore we have omitted it from our review of the evidence.

Choice and segregation in public education
In the case of health, few people are concerned about the distribution of patients across services except in so far as this makes a difference to health outcomes: otherwise, whoever is in the bed next to you does not make much difference to anyone

except you. This is not true of integration in public education which, it is argued, not only leads to better (certainly fairer) educational outcomes, but also brings with it broader social benefits. In so far as extended choice might add up to a more segregated public school community, then, that is one consideration against it. This raises the final, education-specific, question below:

- What effects have school choice policies had on the distribution of students across public schools?

In summary, the six main questions we look to the evidence to address are:

1. where services have offered more choice, have service users taken it up?

2. where choice in public services has been exercised, which people were able to exercise it effectively?

3. do choice schemes result in improved efficiency/quality?

4. do the benefits of efficiency outweigh any additional expenditure, such as that required to generate excess capacity of flexibility in the system?

5. how have any costs and benefits been distributed across services and service users?

6. what effects have school choice policies had on the distribution of students across public schools?

The evidence base
This paper addresses the evidence relevant to these questions. Throughout we have tried to pay as much attention as possible to the policy details that make a difference to these outcomes (for example differences in funding, supply of services, regulation and support for service users in choosing). The paper is intended as a guide to these issues: it is neither exhaustive nor critical. It goes without saying that there are a large number of important methodological difficulties involved in answering the questions above.

Generally our strategy has simply been to assemble the relevant evidence across the academic debate on choice.

However, when looking at the systemic effects of user choice policies we have excluded some material. A large proportion of the studies in this area dedicate themselves exclusively to what happens to an individual when he or she leaves a regular public service provider for a 'choice' option, for example a private provider paid for by the public. If choice policies require us to embrace new forms of provision, then the quality and the efficiency of that provision is certainly crucial. However, the fundamental claim behind the choice of provider model is not just that it benefits those who exercise choice, but that is has a general *levelling-up* effect for all service users. For this reason we leave out studies that only address the question of what happens to 'choosers'. Instead we include studies either that address the overall impact of choice on public services (on 'choosers' and 'non-choosers'), or those studies that address the impact of choice on 'non-choosers' only.

School choice

Summary of findings

1. Contestability under parental choice can work to improve the quality and the efficiency of state schools, given the right policy conditions. This is the conclusion of a large number of the studies looking at school choice. There is a substantial amount of research relating to school choice, in particular on the competitive effects of school choice policies on state schools.

2. The reported effects of targeted voucher schemes in the US are substantial and often apply for disadvantaged and lower-achieving pupils; otherwise the effects of parental choice on state schools are not always large or significant, but are almost without exception not negative (this applies also to those studies that investigate achievement among disadvantaged and low-achieving state school students under schemes that offer choice to all parents).

3. Parental choice policies that have allowed for widespread, overt, selection of pupils by schools have generally reported negative or indifferent results on all counts. In Chile, the parental choice policy that allowed for overt selection of pupils by schools reported negative results on equity in up-take of choice, on the effects of parental choice on state schools, and on segregation. In New Zealand schools have also been given a considerable degree of discretion over admissions for a substantial period, with mixed results at best.

4. In addition to the issue of overt selection, parental choice policies that have allowed independent, or

quasi-independent, bodies to accept state sector per pupil funding have generally reported positive effects on state schools. By contrast, schemes that have confined parental choice (without additional fees) to the state sector without introducing additional capacity through new forms of provision, have in general reported variable, indifferent, or negative results. This is true of the UK, which reports mixed results over time (see below).

5. A crucial question, which is not wholly answered in the evidence, is why this is the case: policy-based explanations include differences in capacity, flexibility and demand-sensitivity, as well as differences in the terms of competition between choice schools and regular state schools.

6. A partial exception to the general rule above is the following: the operation of inter-district or 'Tiebout' choice in the US – which is different in structure to other forms of school choice - is associated consistently with greater achievement and efficiency across regular state schools; in some cases the association is strongest for low-achieving and disadvantaged students.

7. Up-take of choice among parents is generally high; and where choice has been accompanied with new forms of provision there has followed a substantial response on the supply side.

8. Patterns of take-up of choice among different socio-economic groups are different for the various countries: in Sweden, all socio-economic groups have so far been equally likely to attend new choice schools where these have a general educational profile; in the US disadvantaged, minority and low achieving students have in many cases been more likely to attend charter schools, which are often set up with the explicit purpose of catering to these groups.

9. In the UK there is some evidence that schools have responded to the introduction of choice by going in for covert selection and targeting of desired pupils. Take-up of choice by parents (measured in terms of actual pupil movement as well as by various survey and institutional proxies) has, for specific families in specific contexts,

----

in the US disadvantaged, minority and low achieving students have in many cases been more likely to attend charter schools, which are often set up with the explicit purpose of catering to these groups

----

been skewed towards more advantaged families: a marked difference in social class was reported between the minority of parents at the extreme ends of the activity scale; up-take has also been skewed towards more advantaged families in non-urban areas, where there are fewer available alternatives and, importantly, fewer options for travel.

10. Overall in the UK, the use of catchment areas is associated with higher levels of segregation than would be expected, taking into account geographical factors, school number and school type. At the same time there is some evidence to suggest that segregation is reduced in areas where choice has been most effective. In short, it appears that integration may be better served under a system of choice than one of catchment areas and distance-based criteria. At the same time, the use of banding criteria was associated with reduced segregation as compared to either of these options.

11. Parents' choices have caused some schools in the UK to polarise by intake. Again, this was due mainly to non-urban contexts where available alternatives and transport options were more limited, or to schools at the extreme ends of the popularity scale.

12. Studies examining the effect of competition for pupils on state schools in the UK have reached mixed results: those associations that were positive were nevertheless not large. The results have changed over time and it is possible that the situation underlying the measures of competition used has changed (in general these measures rely on school density).

13. The UK has combined choice policies on the demand side with little flexibility on the supply side, which, as a result, has had little scope for responding to parental preferences. In addition the number of school places has declined over time. Flexibility and capacity are therefore two possible explanations for why the results have been less positive than those from countries in which overt selection has been restricted and, importantly, choice has been accompanied by new forms of provision.

School choice: the UK

12 Le Grand, *Motivation, Agency and Public Policy: Of Knights and Knaves, Pawns and Queens* Oxford University Press, New York, 2003
West, A and Pennell, H., 'How New is New Labour? The Quasi-Market and English Schools 1997 to 2001': *British Journal of Educational Studies*, ISSN 0007 – 1005 Vol. 50, No. 2, June 2002, pp 206 – 224

13 Local Authorities were prevented from making further adjustments.

14 Taylor, C., *Geography of the 'New' Education Market: School Choice in England and Wales*, Aldershot: Ashgate, 2002.

15 West, A. and Pennell, H., *Educational Reform and School Choice in England and Wales*, Education Economics, Vol. 5, No. 3, 1997

The policy

Parental choice of school has existed in one form or another in the UK for some time. In the late 1980s the Thatcher government introduced into public education a series of reforms on the 'choice of provider' model outlined in the introduction. These were designed to extend both choice and its financial incentives. The bulk of the reforms were introduced under the 1988 Education Reform Act. Although it has made several adjustments, the Labour government left the school choice reforms largely intact[12].

According to the Act, a large and increasing proportion of funding was taken from LEAs and was instead given directly to schools. At the same time schools were given greater discretion over their use of funding, for example with regards to hire and fire (but not to pay). A substantial proportion of funding was allocated to schools according to the number and age of their pupils, with a small proportion adjusted for other factors, including social deprivation and Special Educational Needs (SEN)[13]: one study estimated that, in 1992, 56% of schools' overall general budget was determined according to the number of pupils at the school[14]. Along with a general programme of devolved funding, schools could also (after a parental ballot) become 'Grant-Maintained', in which case they would opt out of LEA control altogether. Grant Maintained schools received all of their funding directly from central government. Schools were offered (limited) financial incentives to opt out: in 1996 3% of primary school students and 20% of secondary school students were being educated in schools that had opted out of LEA control[15].

Along with the above changes to the financing and autonomy of state schools, parents could express a preference for any school, and they had the right to attend any school with spare places. However the operation of parental choice in practice has differed substantially between LEAs, which have implemented varied – and often fairly complicated – arrangements for: expressing and aggregating parental preferences; for admissions criteria in cases of over-subscription; and for provision of school transport for students[16]. Schools are permitted to use various (published) admissions criteria for allocating scarce places, and, in general, LEAs will only provide transport to the nearest school. The admissions process remains fragmented and is generally regarded as placing considerable costs on parents exercising choice.

There have been a number of restrictions on the supply side of school choice in the UK that have applied both to parental choice and its financial consequences for schools. One of these restrictions has been that independent schools have not been permitted systematically to accept state per pupil funding. In addition, flexibility in the state sector has been restricted by a general policy of rationalisation of school places: schools have not (in theory) been permitted to exceed their Planned Admission Numbers (PAN)[17]; and no school has been allowed to open, or to expand[18] where places remain in nearby schools (Surplus Places Rule). As a result, it is said that the UK has introduced the components of school choice on the demand side, but that there has nevertheless been little scope for demand sensitivity in UK public education[19].

1. Have parents exercised school choice?

There is little overall information on the extent to which parents have exercised choice. Parsons et al. used postcode data to investigate the movements of pupils transferring from year six to seven in one LEA between 1991-2 and 1995-6[20]. In general, the level of parental activity in choosing schools was substantial: they report a progressive rise in the number of pupils attending out of catchment schools during the period – from 33% to 39%. [This overall increase was due largely to movement between comprehensives.] However they report large differences in the level of parental activity between, on the one hand, the three rural catchments (which had a mean export rate of 9%), and, on the other, the 'suburban' area (33%) and

16 White, P et al. 'Regional and Local Differences in Admission Arrangements for Schools', *Oxford Review of Education*, Vol. 27, No. 3, 2001

DfES, Department for Education and Skills *Parents' experience of the process of choosing a secondary school.* London. www.dfes.gov.uk 2001

17 LEA's set PANs for schools, but the 1988 ERA loosened this by imposing admissions levels for schools called the 'standard number'; which were determined by the size of each school's intake in sep 1997 or sep 1998. Coincidentally 1987 was a peak year and so this made more room.

18 At least in the sense that would require, for example, a new building.

19 Le Grand, J. and Dixon, A. *Choice and Equity in the National Health Service,* 2004.

20 Parsons, E et al. 'School Catchments and Pupil movements: a case study in parental choice', *Educational Studies*, Vol. 26, No. 1, 2000

21 Gewirtz et al. *Markets, Choice and Equity in Education*, Buckingham: Open University Press, 1995

22 Blair, M. 'Black Teachers, black students and education markets, *Cambridge journal of education*, 1994, 24(2): 277-91
For suggestive evidence that choice has, in general, disadvantaged minorities see: Tomlinson, S., Diversity, Choice and Ethnicity: the effects of educational markets on ethnic minorities (1997) *Oxford Review of Education, Vol. 23, No. 1.*

23 Raab, G. and Adler, M. 'A tale of two cities: The impact of parental choice on admissions to primary schools in Edinburgh and Dundee', in Bondi, L. and Mathews, M.H. (eds). *Education and Society*, Routledge: London, 1994, pp. 113 - 147

'more varied' area (39%). It is not clear that this situation is representative, however. The situation has also changed over time: for example the number of surplus places in the UK has decreased over the period since choice was introduced.

2. Which parents have exercised choice of school in the UK?

School choice policies bring with them the worry that more advantaged families will be able to monopolise new choices. This is in part because school choice policies in the UK are associated historically with policies that allow for overt selection of pupils by schools. However there are two additional concerns, which are attached more firmly to the issue of choice. The first is that school choice policies extend both the means and the motive for schools to go in for covert – as well as overt – selection of desired pupils. The second is that – whatever schools do – there exist decisive social and financial constraints on parents in exercising choice of school. Both of these, it is argued, may work to ensure that new school choices are monopolised by more advantaged families.

There is a limited amount of *direct* evidence to suggest that choice has encouraged schools in the UK to go in for covert selection of pupils. Most notably, Gewirtz et al. examine the operation of school choice in three contiguous LEAs in the years 1991 to 1994[21]. On the basis of a variety of sources, including interviews, they conclude that schools in these LEAs responded to the introduction of choice by targeting students who were more able, motivated and committed (particularly girls from middle class and South Asian backgrounds). This was despite there being no overt selection in their admissions policies. Similarly, Blair presents evidence that schools have responded to the introduction of choice by discriminating against black students and groups[22].

Studies have also addressed directly the issue of social and financial constraints on exercising school choice. A group of such studies relate the characteristics of parents to their activity in choosing schools, as measured for example by their answers to surveys. For example, Raab and Adler find that parents who placed official requests for a choice of school not originally allocated to them tended to be higher up the socio-economic scale[23]. Carrol and Walford relate social status to an extensive set of criteria designating the 'active chooser': a significant minority of working-class parents did count as active; however parents from higher social classes were more likely to be judged active[24]. Finally Taylor reports that, of the 3% of 200 parents in 1995-6 who reported considering more than four schools, private or university-educated parents were over-represented[25]. The level of variation among the other 97% of parents was relatively low.

A further approach, which amalgamates issues of selection of pupils by schools with the issue of constraints on choosing, is to investigate the extent to which students from different socio-economic groups have *actually moved* among public schools under choice policy in the UK. For example, Parsons et al. used postcode data to investigate the movements of pupils transferring from year six to seven in one LEA between 1991-2 and 1995-6[26]. Parsons et al. suggest that take-up of choice by parents has been equitable. However this is on the rather limited grounds that, among the parents choosing out-of-catchment schools, parents living in 'struggling' and 'aspiring' neighbour-hoods were over-represented. [The result depended anyway on the local context, such as whether or not the area was an urban one, which suggests that up-take of choice by parents in non-urban areas may not just be lower, but may also be more skewed by social class.]

By contrast, an early and influential study of pupil movement in Scotland reported that choice has been skewed by socio-economic status. Willms et al. relied on survey answers from 5000 pupils in Fife, as well as 616 parents in 3 LEAs, in reporting that students who moved to schools other than their local were – to a varying extent - more likely to have parents with higher levels of education and more prestigious occupations. Similarly, in Stillman conducted a survey of 1,792 parents in the UK and found, on the basis of distance travelled, that parents more active in choosing schools were likely to be university graduates and successful professionally[27].

Perhaps the most detailed examination of this issue is Taylor (2002), who relates pupils' social status to the probability that they will attend each of the various schools available to them[28]. He relies on postcode data for just over 30,000 pupils transferring to secondary school in the 1995-6 school year,

24 Carrol, S and Walford, G. 'Parents' responses to the school quasi-market', Research Papers in Education, 1997, vol. 12. 1:pp. 32 - 36

25 Taylor, C. Geography of the 'New' Education Market: School Choice in England and Wales, Aldershot: Ashgate, 2002

26 Parsons, E. et al. 'School Catchments and Pupil movements: a case study in parental choice', Educational Studies, 2000

27 Stillman, A. 'Legislating for choice', in Flude M. and Hammer, M. (eds) The Education Reform Act 1988: Its origins and Implications, Lewes: Falmer, 1999

28 Taylor, C. Geography of the 'New' Education Market: School Choice in England and Wales, 2002

along with household survey evidence from just over 200 respondents. He reports that parents and children across all social groups exercised choice to some extent, but in some cases activity was skewed towards families at the high end of the socio-economic scale. This was due mainly to a minority of active parents, together with a minority of parents who were especially *inactive* in the context of general activity. The contrast in social status between these two sets of consumers was quite marked. In addition, take-up of choice by families was more skewed by socio-economic status in non-urban areas, with fewer available alternatives and transport options.

In summary, there is local evidence, particularly in the London area, that schools have responded to the introduction of parental choice by covertly selecting desired pupils. In addition, a number of studies have related measures of parental activity in choosing schools to various measures of socio-economic status: these report that active exercise of choice (of course, all parents in the UK make a formal, or 'default' choice) has been skewed towards more advantaged families. In short, there is evidence to support both the worry that the form of choice introduced in UK schools encourages schools to go in for covert selection and the worry that social and financial constraints on making good choices will skew take-up in favour of more advantaged parents. These constraints on choice of schools for disadvantaged families apparently relate both to resources, such as transport, and also to differences in information and motivation between families. With regards to informational and motivational differences, it should be noted that procedures through which parents express choice of school are currently fragmented and in many cases impose considerable costs on parents.

The relationship between socio-economic status and activity in choosing schools is presumably not simply linear. Both the extent of the problem and the possibility of effective solutions depend on the how widely these differences in activity apply, and for which contexts. Taylor suggests that take-up is skewed, but for a 'minority' of families at the more extreme ends of the socio-economic scale. For those families in between, take-up has been more representative; in some contexts families with lower socio-economic status have been over-represented. In addition, take-up has been more likely to be skewed towards more advantaged parents in non-urban areas, with fewer available alternatives, and transport may be a decisive factor in these contexts.

29 Gorard, S. Fitz, J. and Taylor, C. *Schools, Markets and Choice Policies*, London: Routledge Falmer, 2003

3. What has been the effect of school on choice on segregation in public schools?

A common criticism of school choice policies is that they lead to increased segregation on dimensions such as ability, socio-economic status and ethnicity. The most intuitive explanation for why this might occur is that more advantaged families will use their monopoly on choice to cluster into better schools. However it is important to note that this is not the only explanation. The issue of segregation is separable in practice from issues of equity in up-take and selection of pupils by schools. In the US, for example, there is evidence that minority and low socio-economic status students have been more likely to exercise choice of charter school, but have thereby segregated *themselves* within them (see the US section).

The evidence cited as relevant to school choice and segregation in the UK falls into two general classes. On the one hand, there is general evidence on the overall pattern of segregation between state schools over the period since the 1988 ERA was introduced (but not, unfortunately, for a significant period *before* it was introduced). On the other hand there is evidence that relates changes in segregation more closely to education policy – in some cases to the operation of parental choice.

The overall pattern of segregation since the 1988 ERA

Gorard, Taylor and Fitz have conducted an extensive and influential research programme on the extent and causes of segregation for state schools in England and Wales[29]. Primarily, segregation is measured as the number of pupils that would have to change schools for there to be an equal distribution between schools of children eligible for free school meals. Less extensive data on race, SEN and English as a first language are also used: in general the results are repeated. At the top level the sample includes data for every state-funded school in England and Wales.

They report two patterns in overall segregation by

30 Gibson, A. and Asthana, S., ' What's in a number? Commentary on Gorard and Fitz's 'Investigating the determinants of segregation between schools'' *Research Papers in Education,* 1999, 15(2): 133-54; Noden, P 'Rediscovering the impact of marketisation: dimensions of social segregation in England's secondary schools 1994 – 1999', *British journal of Sociology of Education* 21(23): 271 – 90. This may be thought a rather cursory treatment of these studies. However the disagreement between, on the one hand, Gorard et al., and these (and other) authors is complex and involves a great many clarifications and alleged retractions. We believe that the best compromise is probably the statement above.

31 This was after a short-term increase in segregation in some areas in the year 1990-91. The authors have suggested that this may be a 'starting gun effect', where more advantaged families are able to monopolise choice in the period before most families become familiar with the process.

32 For a summary of the various disputes from the *authors* of the project, see: http://www.cardiff.ac.uk/socsi/m arkets/Papers/FinalESRCreport. pdf

socio-economic status over the period of the study. Along with several well-known studies of segregation in UK education[30], they find that segregation increased annually between 1995 and 2001, in their estimation from 30% to 33%. [1995 was the first year in which all compulsory secondary school students had enrolled since the introduction of the reforms.] On the other hand, they also report that segregation decreased between 1989 and 1995 from a *high* of 35% in January 1989 – a year they take as giving a snapshot of segregation in the UK before choice actually became effective[31]. They conclude that choice has not single-handedly exacerbated segregation over the period since school choice was introduced.

The study has been subject to some methodological criticism[32]. Initially criticism focussed on the proper indices of segregation – an objection that more recently appears to have been abandoned, and replaced instead with disagreements over the use of free school meal eligibility in estimating segregation. Taking the results at face value, it is clear that choice has not single-handedly exacerbated overall segregation in UK public education. On the other hand, the authors take care to emphasize that a primary result of their study is that the contribution of choice, and indeed education policy more generally, to overall segregation should not be over-estimated. Indeed, they report both that their explanatory model explains 100% of segregation as they measure it, and that 90% is explained in terms of extra-educational factors, such as residential segregation.

For this reason they conclude that the overall result may not tell us much about the impact of choice – in either direction - on segregation: any effort to determine the effect that parental choice has had on segregation in the UK needs to relate segregation more directly to education policy and to parental choice.

The relation of segregation to areas of education policy

Within education policy (i.e. within that 10% boundary of explanation) Gorard et al. report factors that are related to parental choice, but which are not strictly identical, and which have a *more significant* effect on segregation than parental choice per se. They report hat the nature and number of local

With regard to the nature of local schools, selective, fee-paying, voluntary-aided and grant-maintained schools are all associated with higher levels of segregation

33 Fitz, J., Gorard, S. and Taylor, C. *Diversfying public education or creating a two-tier system? Lessons from England*, presentation at AERA annual conference, New Orleans, April 2002

schools has a significant effect on segregation within LEAs. A greater number of surplus places are associated with greater integration, as is school closure, which appears to have the effect of bringing different pupils together. It is not clear whether any changes in these over the period should be attributed to the operation of choice, as these are affected also by e.g. the on-going rationalisation of school places by LEAs.

With regard to the nature of local schools, selective, fee-paying, voluntary-aided and grant-maintained schools are all associated with higher levels of segregation. This suggests that the nature of the supply side under the parental choice policy in the UK has been important in determining segregation. What is less clear, unfortunately, is exactly *why* these schools are associated with increased segregation. The authors themselves are unsure whether it is 'diversity or selection' that is the primary cause; however they point out that what all of these school have in common is the facility to recruit widely against schools with narrow catchment areas[33].

Gorard et al. suggest that – *after* the factors above – LEAs' general admission procedures have a tangible effect on segregation. Alongside a population bulge in the number of children of secondary school age, LEAs have reduced the number of surplus places over the years through a program of re-organisation and rationalisation. This means that schools are increasingly likely to become over-subscribed and consequently the use of admissions criteria has increased. There is significant variation in admissions criteria, which include parental or sibling connection, proximity, catchment areas, difficult journey elsewhere, feeder or linked schools, first choice or strong request, age, single sex or religion, medical, social or special educational need, banding criteria and suitability to the school's ethos or focus.

34 West, A. and Hind, A., *Secondary school admissions in England: Exploring the extent of overt and covert selection*, Centre for Educational Research, Department of Social Policy, London School of Economics and Political Science, 2003

35 Various reports of a house price premium: Gibbons and Machin (2003) 'Valuing English Primary Schools', *Journal of Urban Economics* 53(2); Rosenthal, R. 'The value of secondary school quality', *Oxford Bulletin of Economics and Statistics, 65, 3 2003*; D. Leech & E. Campos, 'Is comprehensive education really free? A case study of the effects of secondary school admissions policies on house prices in one local area', *Warwick Economic; Research Papers, no.581*; Royal Institution of Chartered Surveyors, Press Release 03/10/03, 'Premium on houses in "good" school catchment areas vary across England and Wales'.

36 "Gorard, S., Fitz, J. and Taylor, C. *Schools, Markets and Choice Policies*, London, 2003"

37 Hardman, J and Levacic, R., 'The Impact of Competition on Secondary Schools' in Glatter et al. (eds.) *Choice and Diversity in Schooling: perspectives and prospects*: Routledge. 1997

38 Gorard, S., Questioning the crisis account: a review of evidence for increasing polarisation in schools, *Educational Research Vol. 42 No. 3 2000 309-321*

39 Bradley, S. and Taylor, J., *The Effect of the Quasi-Market on the Efficiency-Equity Trade-off in the Secondary School Sector*, Lancaster University Management School Working Paper 2000/008

Alongside siblings and medical or social need, the most commonly used criteria are distance from the school, which is used by 86% of secondary schools in England, and catchment areas – used by 69% of English secondary schools[34]. A number of commentators have suggested that the use of catchment areas exacerbates segregation. This is on the grounds that they act to lock in local patterns of segregation, and that they encourage a mutually determining connection between house prices and school quality[35]. Gorard et al. find support for the view that catchment areas can exacerbate segregation: use of catchment areas by LEAs is associated with higher levels of segregation – about twice what they would expect, other things being equal. At the same time, use of banding criteria by LEAs is associated with levels of segregation running at about half of what would be expected, other things being equal[36].

The relation of segregation to parental choice

The results of studies looking directly at the relation of segregation to the current system of choice have reached mixed conclusions. There is evidence to suggest that parental choice in the UK has worked in line with exam results and evaluations, and that poorly performing schools in particular have experienced limited falls in their pupil rolls[37]. Often, the same studies present suggestive evidence that schools more successful in terms of exam results and recruitment have experienced declines in the proportion of pupils eligible for free school meals, although there is disagreement on whether this has happened to a significant extent[38]. Nevertheless, this has raised the worry in the UK – often put by sceptics of school choice policies – that school choice leads not only to segregation, but to polarisation by intake of better and worse-performing schools.

Two studies set out to examine the impact of the current model of school choice on segregation by *ability*. Bradley et al. found that schools with improved performance experienced a reduction in their proportion of pupils eligible for free school meals, with schools with poor exam results experiencing the reverse[39]. More recently, in an unpublished presentation, Propper et al. report that an increase in the number of schools, or in the number of 'good' schools, in a 10-minute 'Drive

Time Zone' is associated with a decrease in the variability of ability within schools as compared to those within the same competition space[40].

Taylor investigates the contribution of parental choice to polarisation of schools by *socio-economic* intake[41]. He relates changes in the enrolment of schools to the movement of pupils transferring from primary to secondary school in eight representative LEAs. He reports a complex conclusion. On the one hand choice apparently *has* lead to polarisation by intake of some schools; on the other, the overall effect of pupils' movements under parental choice was apparently greater integration by socio-economic status. The direction of the result was influenced importantly by the *context* in which choice was taking place.

The positive effect of choice on integration generally applied for fairly attractive schools, with average exam results. On the other hand, Taylor reports that there were a number of schools at the top and bottom end of the quality spectrum whose intakes comprised students from more and more prosperous (top) and more and more disadvantaged backgrounds (bottom). For the most attractive schools, this was brought about by especially active parents, with high levels of social and cultural capital. In the least attractive schools it was due more to a combination of parents with relatively low levels of social and cultural capital, who did not participate in choice, as well as a number of more advantaged parents who sent their children elsewhere.

In these cases, it appears that basic differences between families in terms activity and efficacy in making choices has, as critics suggest, contributed to polarisation of school by socio-economic intake. In addition, Taylor reports that polarisation was more likely to take place in non-urban areas, with fewer available alternatives and options for transport. On a 'pessimistic' estimate, 38% of the schools studied polarised to some extent by intake; however Taylor suggests that in reality the number that polarised 'significantly' was smaller than this suggests. The majority of schools that polarised by intake were from the bottom rather then the top tier.

In summary, the relative contribution of choice to segregation (and education policy more generally) is small

40 Burgess, S, McConnell B, Propper C and Wilson D, *Sorting and Choice in English Secondary Schools*, CMPO, Bristol University, October 2004 draft

41 Taylor, C. *Geography of the 'New' Education Market: School Choice in England and Wales*, 2002

as compared to those determinants of segregation that lie outside education policy. Judging by the measure of overall socio-economic segregation employed, choice has not single-handedly exacerbated segregation in the UK; however, by itself, this leaves the relation between choice and segregation fairly indeterminate.

All other things being equal, the use of catchment areas is associated with greater segregation and the use of banding criteria is associated with decreased segregation. Finally, segregation is sensitive to the nature of local schools. It is not yet clear exactly why this is so, although it is plausible that selection is a factor. Whatever the exact explanation, segregation under choice has clearly been sensitive to the make-up of the supply side, and this is an important policy point for the issue of choice and segregation.

Those studies that relate school composition more directly to parental choice have reached mixed conclusions. There is some evidence that parental choice has lead to increased stratification by ability: it appears that schools have experienced decreases in the proportion of students eligible for Free School Meals at the same time as making gains on exam results - and vice versa; another study found that greater school density is associated with a decrease in the variability of ability between schools.

On segregation by socio-economic status, a smaller-scale study reports both that students' movements under choice have worked to decrease segregation overall, and that they

----

There is some evidence that parental choice has lead to increased stratification by ability: it appears that schools have experienced decreases in the proportion of students eligible for Free School Meals at the same time as making gains on exam results – and vice versa

----

have caused some schools to polarise by socio-economic intake. That some polarisation should have occurred is consistent with studies reporting that activity in exercising choice has been skewed towards more advantaged families. In general, polarisation has been due to parents at the more extreme ends of the activity scale, and has taken place in schools at the more extreme ends of the achievement scale - particularly in poorly performing schools. Where polarisation has occurred, it appears that the central causes have been brute differences in motivation between parents and differential access to transport and available alternatives in non-urban areas.

4. What has been the effect of choice on academic standards and efficiency in schools; and how have any costs or benefits in these areas been distributed across different pupils?

As with the debate on choice and segregation, the evidence relevant to standards and efficiency either gives a general account of changes in exam results over the period post 1988, or attempts to relate educational outcomes more directly to parental choice. Studies from both categories are presented below.

Overall changes in exam results

There is disagreement within the literature on how exam results have changed over the period since school choice was introduced in the UK. Commentators tend to agree that, on average, exam results have improved: instead the controversy is over the performance of students at the bottom of the achievement scale.

In an early study covering the years 1992 to 1996, West and Pennel report that the average point score of pupils at GCSE and GNVQ improved over the period. However they also report evidence of polarisation by achievement: the score for the top tenth of pupils increased by 7%; the score for the bottom tenth fell by 13%. Similarly, a study by Gibson and Asthana reports a widening gap in performance at GCSE between the top and bottom 10% of English *schools* over the period 1994 to 1998. Gorard et al. have raised doubts about these results, on the grounds that they report percentage point differences without accounting properly for the size of the underlying figures from which they are derived[42]. Using an

42 Gorard, S., Fitz, J. and Taylor, C. *Schools, Markets and Choice Policies*, London, 2003
Gorard, S., 'Questioning the crisis account: a review of evidence for increasing polarisation in schools', 2000

With reference to the national attainment tests, two objections are summarised in Le Grand, J. First, the International Association for the Evaluation of Educational Achievements administered an alternative test in 1999 to a national sample of secondary school children age 13. Maths and science scores in 1999 did not show up as statistically different to those of 1995. However the range of skills measured is different, and - in contrast to the national assessment tests - children and teachers faced minimal incentives to achieve on the test. Second, and similarly, un-published results from the university of Durham found little improvement for year-six pupils in reading skills from 1999 to 2002 and in vocabulary between 1997 and 2002. On the other hand, they assess only reading, while the national tests also assess writing, spelling and handwriting. Moreover, the same team did find improvements in science (5%), and maths (9%), between 1997 and 2002. [QCA (2001) Five-Year Review of Standards Reports: Summary, Qualifications and Curriculum Authority: www.qca.uk; Schagen, I. and Morrison, J. QUASE Quantitative Analysis for Self-Evaluation: Overview Report 1997: Analysis of GCSE cohorts 1994 to 1996, Slough: NfER, 1998

43 Gorard, S., 'Questioning the Crisis Account: a review of evidence for increasing polarisation in schools', 2000 and Gorard et al, *Schools, Markets and Choice Policies*, 2003

44 Glennerster, H (2002) 'United Kingdom education' *Oxford Review of Economic Policy* 18:120-136

45 Le Grand, *Motivation, Agency and Public Policy: Of Knights and Knaves, Pawns and Queens*, 2003

46 This is particularly true for the GCSE results. For the case against see: Tymms, P and Fitz-Gibbon, C. (2001) 'Standards, achievement and educational performance: a cause for celebration?' in R. Phillips and J. Furlong (eds) *Education, Reform and the State: Twenty-five Years of Politics, Policy and Practice*, London: RoutledgeFalmer. For some limited defence of GCSEs over time see: QCA (2001) *Five-Year Review of Standards Reports: Summary*, Qualifications and Curriculum Authority: www.qca.uk; Schagen, I and Morrison, J. QUASE *Quantitative Analysis for Self-Evaluation: Overview Report 1997: Analysis of GCSE cohorts 1994 to 1996*, Slough: NfER, 1998

alternative method for aggregating the results, they argue instead that, although a large gap remains, GCSE attainment for the lowest achievers has improved over the period 1989 – 2001 and that (slightly artificially) the gap between the highest and lowest achievers has narrowed[43].

In an influential study Howard Glennerster discovers similar trends in the national attainment tests, which he uses to assess indirectly the effects of the quasi market[44](per pupil spending and average class sizes remained roughly static over the period and so the results are taken as indicating the *efficiency* of state schools). The tests were introduced fully in 1995 and are taken by all pupils at ages 7, 11, 14 and 16, in Maths, English and Science. Glennerster finds that the percentage of pupils reaching a given level of achievement rose steadily over the period. The occasional blip aside, this applies for all subjects, at all levels and across all five years. The lowest-performing schools showed the greatest improvements by 2001, and the same was true when schools were ranked according to the wealth of the area.

All of these results, including the more positive results, have generated some controversy. A central objection has been that the 'closing gap' effect reported in the later studies is less an indication of greater equality than it is an indication of the limits on improvement for high achievers. [This would of course still leave improvements for low achievers.] In addition the credibility of the exam results themselves has been called into question. 'There are anecdotal accounts of teaching to the test and even of outright fraud'[45]. Moreover it has been suggested that the results may be the artefacts of deficiencies or changes in the nature of assessment[46].

Acknowledging the assessment problem, Gorard and Taylor attempt a 'preliminary' consideration of the effects of the choice reforms by comparing the performance of state-funded schools with the fee-paying sector - the reasoning being that although the ERA reforms only impacted on the state sector, any changes in the nature of assessment would have affected both sectors equally. They find that GCSE results have indeed risen relative to the fee-paying sector (and as above, that the gap between top and bottom overall has closed). They acknowledge the possibility of a 'ceiling effect'. In addition they are fairly agnostic on the extent to which choice was the cause of any improvements. As with the issue of segregation, if we take the positive results at face value then we reach the conclusion that low achievers have improved in exams under a policy of parental choice. However the precise relation of choice to any improvements remains unclear.

Glennerster addresses the issue of resources for state schools, finding that per pupil spending and class sizes remained roughly static over the period 1995 to 2001. However, it is also argued that outcomes may be part of a longer-term trend[47], or the result of any of the numerous policy initiatives introduced over the period. Importantly the Numeracy and Literacy hours were introduced over the period and there is evidence – along with a widespread belief – that these have contributed substantially to improvements[48]. In addition, there is also the possibility that those policies that naturally accompany choice, but which may nevertheless be implemented separately – such as assessment or flexibility for schools – may have made their own contribution to improvements[49]. For these reasons, and again, if we are to get beyond the conclusion that the introduction of choice has not single-handedly counteracted a general trend towards equity in exam results, we have to try and relate changes in standards more directly to the operation of parental choice.

The relation of performance and efficiency to school choice

A number of studies have attempted to do just this, with mixed results. Levaèiæ relates longitudinal data from over 300 schools taken between 1990 and 1998 to two different measures of competition: the first takes in a variety of structural data to determine the number of schools within an 'Appropriate Area of Competition'; the second is a measure of 'perceived' competition, which is based on the opinions of headmasters collected by Levaèiæ in survey and interviews[50]. She finds that one measure of 'perceived' competition – five or more 'perceived' competitors – is consistently associated with improvements of between 4 and 5.5 percentage points in the percentage of pupils obtaining five or more GCSEs at A* to C by the end of the period. By contrast, the density measure of school choice (number of schools within an AAC) had so significant impact on performance[51].

47 Heath, A. 'The political arithmetic tradition in the sociology of education', *Oxford Review of Education*, 2000, 26(3&4): 313-31

48 Machin, S. and McNally, S. *The literacy hour* (2004) IZA Discussion Paper no. 1005

49 For example: '... professionals dislike being low down on a league table, even if they are not losing custom as a consequence; and this on its own can act as a pressure to lever up performance.'

50 Levaèiæ, R. *An analysis of competition and its impact on educational outcomes*, Occasional Paper No. 34 National Center for the Study of Privatization in Education Teachers College, Columbia University, 2001

51 No competition variable - structural or subjective - had any impact on the number of pupils gaining five or more pass grades (A* - E) at GCSE, although 85% of schools in general did improve on this measure over the period.

52 Le Grand, J *Motivation, Agency and Public Policy: Of Knights and Knaves, Pawns and Queens*, 2003

Schools are judged more or less efficient depending on their attendance rate and their proportion of GCSE grades A * – C*

An influential study by Bradley et al. relates the relative efficiency of all schools in England to the number of schools of different types within a two-kilometre radius. The period studied is 1993 to 1997. Schools are judged more or less efficient depending on their attendance rate and their proportion of GCSE grades A* - C, taking into account the proportion of students on free school meals and the proportion of qualified staff, along with various characteristics of the schools (including whether or not they are selective), their funding, and their local areas or authority. The association is not large, but Bradley finds that the greater degree of competition schools faced, the greater their relative efficiency. There is also some suggestive evidence that the schools with the lowest relative efficiencies in 1993 tended to gain the most over the period.

In a later study Bradley and Taylor reach a similar result for the period 1993 to 1999. This time they use individual data from the Youth Cohort Study for England and Wales, as well as school-level data. Efficiency is now the proportion of pupils attaining five or more GCSEs at A* - C, taking into account the proportion of full time staff, while competition is measured in terms of lagged response to exam performance in other schools. The competition measure is associated positively with school performance and school efficiency (although, again, the effects are small). The effect was twice as large in metropolitan areas.

These last micro-studies of the effects of choice on efficiency 'suggest that at least some of the [overall] efficiency improvements can be directly attributed to the competitive pressures arising from the operation of the quasi-market'[52]. However, more recently, in an unpublished presentation Propper et al. reach a less positive conclusion. They use data from the period 1996 through to 2001 to relate the number of schools within a defined area to exam performance – measured in terms of value-added. They report either a negative or an indifferent association between school density and exam performance. In selective LEAs the number of schools, as well as the number of 'good' schools, within a 10-minute 'Drive Time Zone' had no association with the value-added measure of performance in exams. In comprehensive LEAs there was a negative association. As above, the measure of choice was also associated with increased segregation by ability within schools[53].

In summary, then, overall changes in exam results show improvements for lower-achieving students over the period since the 1998 ERA. A slightly artificial by-product is that the gap in achievement on exams has closed over the period. State schools have improved on exams relative to the fee-paying sector and their resources appear to have remained roughly constant over the period. Choice has therefore not interrupted a trend towards greater equity in exam achievement; however the relation of parental choice to these improvements is unclear.

Several studies have attempted to relate parental choice to both achievement and efficiency in public schools. In general the proxy for parental choice and competition is the *density* of schools within a given area. These studies report fairly small, and mixed, effects. In the light of small effects – in any direction – it should be kept in mind that school choice in the UK has operated with a number of constraints on the responsiveness of the supply side and with a decline in the number of surplus places since 1988. A reported, positive, association between competition and efficiency was strongest in metropolitan areas.

53 At present the paper is in unpublished draft form as a result of a power-point presentation on a related topic, found at: http://www.bris.ac.uk/Depts/CMPO/events/workshops/education2/education2main.htm, and is still being revised. Burgess, S, McConnell B, Propper C and Wilson D, *Sorting and Choice in English Secondary Schools* CMPO, Bristol University, October 2004 draft

School choice: the US

The various forms of school choice in the US

54 Charter schools are essentially de-regulated public schools: various bodies make a commitment to meet the goals set out in their charter; in exchange they receive public funding and a degree of flexibility. Beyond this, charter schools vary a great deal (see below).

55 *Conditional* school choice in the US, as embodied in the NCLBA, is a major practical inspiration for Tony Wright and Pauline Ngan's suggested 'Public Service Guarantees' [Wright, T and Ngan, P., 'A new social contract: from targets to rights in public services', Fabian Ideas 610, The Fabian Society 2004]

School choice operates in a variety of different forms in the US, many of which have been studied. Choice through the housing market, or 'Tiebout' choice, is generally acknowledged as the most influential, and the most commonly exercised, form of parental choice in the US. However, parental choice also operates in the US through charter schools, private schools, voucher, and open enrolment policies[54]. Choice is also likely to expand throughout the US as a result of the federal No Child Left Behind Act (NCLBA), which exposes schools failing to make 'Adequate Yearly Progress' (AYP) to various forms of corrective action, including parental choice[55]. These different forms of choice in the US have produced a large number of evaluative studies, which are reviewed below. Some of these look at the effects on public schools of 'traditional' forms of school choice – choice of private school and choice through the housing market. These impose different costs on schools and parents than other forms of choice (see below), but are nevertheless included. The studies of voucher policies have been particularly influential in the debate on school choice within the UK, particularly for those advocating choice on left-wing grounds.

Two forms of choice in the US – open enrolment between regular public schools and choice through the housing market – are unique in that they do not involve variation on the supply side: parental choice in these cases is between regular public schools (although it may be across administrative, fiscal and legal boundaries). By contrast, charter schools, voucher policies and private school choice all involve additional forms of provision. Since it is an important question whether – and under what conditions – parental choice might be effective purely within the state sector, we were disappointed not to have uncovered any studies of open enrolment policies in the US, which are sometimes designed to introduce contestability between public schools. However there are a large number of studies on the effect on public schools of choice through the housing market. These come with caveats attached, in particular that the operation of 'Tiebout' choice in the US is mediated by the American system of public school finance, which relies heavily on local property taxes. Nevertheless, they may prove interesting on the issue of parental choice within the public sector.

It is arguable that, of the forms of choice in the US which have been studied (so excluding open enrolment policies); only charter schools are relevant to issues of equity in take-up of choice by parents, and to issues of segregation. Voucher policies in the US generally restrict choice to a sub-set of disadvantaged students, which will clearly have an effect on these issues. Moreover, targeted choice policies of this kind have traditionally been dismissed in the UK as inherently limited and divisive (although the idea of restricting choice to students in failing *schools* has recently been mooted): for this reason we exclude information on take-up and segregation for voucher policies and look only at their competitive effects on public schools. Inter-district choice and private school choice, by contrast, are formally open to all comers; however it is clear that they impose larger costs on parents and pupils than choices that do not require parents to pay fees or to move house (they also impose weaker incentives on schools – see below). For these reasons, we have excluded information on take-up and segregation for these, and have again only looked at studies relating to their competitive impact on public schools.

All of the studies below are cited as revealing the effects of competition on public schools, and for that reason they are all included here. However it is only for charter schools – dealt with first – that we include information on take-up and segregation.

Charter Schools

Charter schools are public schools established through contracts, either with a state agency or a local school board. They are run by a variety of different entities, from for-profit organisations to parents - the point being that flexibility is traded in return for public funding and a commitment to meet the goals and requirements set out in the charter.

Charters are subject to the same rules on church-state relations and discrimination as public schools. They are not permitted to charge fees, nor are they allowed to select students by ability.

Charter schools vary a great deal, and beyond the above characterisation it is not clear that much can be said about them that is both general and useful. This has been a problem particularly for those studies evaluating the performance of charter schools – especially because they have such different social and pedagogical emphases. It is also a problem for anyone relying on charter schools in general to get an idea of the effects on equity in up-take, on segregation, and on competitive effects on public schools. Ideally, an investigation of these issues would relate each result to its particular circumstances. We have attempted this to some extent, particularly for the issue of competition, however to do so fully would take up too much time and space. For this reason it is worth emphasising at this point the variations that exist between charter school policies, both *within* and between states.

The type of students that choose charter schools, the effect of charter schools on segregation, and the competitive effects of charter schools on public schools will depend on a number of different features, many of which apply also to voucher policies. These include:

- the social and pedagogical emphasis of the charter schools

- charter schools' admissions criteria

- the proportion of students within a given area that attend charter schools

- the total number of charter schools that can be created and the total proportion of students allowed to attend them

- whether or not charter schools can be newly created or converted from existing public or private schools

- the body that approves charter schools and their funding

- the availability of start-up, planning, or facilities funding

- the proportion of funding that follows students to charter schools

- which groups are permitted to set up charter schools
- the way in which the political process plays out in support for public schools in competition with charter schools.

Keeping these factors in mind, we now examine the evidence on charter schools that relates to our four questions.

1. Have parents exercised choice of charter school?

We have encountered little *detailed* research on the expansion of charter schools, and in particular on the areas in which they are most likely to be established (again, this in fact varies). Across the US in 2002-02, 1.2% of students were enrolled in a total of 2,348 charter schools. The largest enrolments by state were: District of Columbia (9.2%), Arizona – called the 'Wild West' of charter school regulation (6.7%)[56], Michigan (3.8%), Colorado (3.3%) and California (2.2%)[57].

2. Which parents have been more likely to exercise choice of charter schools?

There are a large number of state-specific evaluations of charter school schemes that relate to issues of choice and segregation. In general these offer static, cross-sectional comparisons of the racial or socio-economic make-up of charter schools compared to conventional public schools in a given state or local area (and so are used both to assess whether choice has been skewed towards particular families and to assess the contribution of charter schools to segregation). Neither is a perfect measure and they can mask large under-lying differences between schools. Unsurprisingly, these state-level studies tend to reach different conclusions, related closely to the circumstances of the schools.

As above, it is difficult to reach any *general* conclusion here. Returning to the five states above, there is evidence to suggest: that charter schools in Columbia are not creaming the top pool of applicants[58]; that charter schools in Arizona are not either[59] but that they are selecting white students and are responsible for a 2% drop in the proportion of these students in conventional public schools[60]; that Michigan charter schools serve a greater proportion of minorities than either the state or their local districts[61], but (on the basis of half of their charter

56 Dee, T. and Fu, H . 'Do Charter Schools Skim Students or Drain Resources?' *Economics of Education* Review, 2004, 23: 259-271

57 NCES, Common Core of Data, 2001-02; ECS. All but California and the District of Columbia also offer some form of open enrolment scheme; Arizona and Colorado have mandatory inter-district schemes.

58 Henig, J., Moser, M., Holyoke, T. and Lacireno-Paquet, N. *Making a Choice, Making a Difference? An Evaluation of Charter Schools in the District of Columbia,* The Center for Washington Area Studies, The George Washington University November, 1999

59 Solmon, L. Garcia, D. and Paark K. Does *Charter School Attendance Improve Test Scores? The Arizona Results,* The Goldwater Institute, March 2001

60 Dee, T and Fu, H . 'Do Charter Schools Skim Students or Drain Resources?', 2004. This is one of few studies that actually examine the movement of pupils over time.

61 *Michigan's Charter School Initiative: From Theory to Practice, Public Sector Consultants* (Inc.and MAX-IMUS, Inc. for the Michigan Department of Education): February 1999

62 Miron, G, & Nelson, C.
*What's public about charter
schools: Lessons learned about
school choice and
accountability.* Thousand Oaks,
CA: Corwin Press, 2002

63 *The State of Charter
Schools in Colorado* 2001-02,
Colorado Department of
Education), March 2003

64 *The State of Charter
Schools in Colorado*, 1999-
2000: 'The Characteristics,
Status and Performance Record
of Colorado Charter Schools',
Colorado Department of
Education: March 2001

65 *Colorado Charter Schools
Evaluation Study: The
Characteristics, Status and
Performance Record of
Colorado Charter Schools*,
Colorado Department of
Education: January 2000

66 Raymond M. *The
Performance of California
Charter Schools*, CREDO/Hoover
Institution: May 2003

67 *Charter School Operations
and Performance: Evidence
from California*, RAND
Corporation: June 2003

68 Reported in: Hoxby, C.,
'School choice and school
competition: Evidence from
the United States', *Swedish
Economic Policy Review*, 2003

69 Hoxby, C. 'School choice
and school competition:
Evidence from the United
States', *Swedish Economic
Policy Review*, 2003

schools) serve a slightly lower percentage of low-income students than their surrounding districts[62]; that Colorado charter schools in general tend to enrol fewer minority and poor students[63] and tend not to reflect the diversity of public schools in the state as a whole[64] [65]; and finally that California charter schools serve a higher proportion of lower-performing students[66], along with a roughly equal proportion of black and Hispanic students[67].

Some studies have focused specifically on the question of whether students are more likely to enrol in charter schools if they are high or low achievers. Hanushek, Rivkin et al. use data for Texas to look at future charter school students' achievement while they were in public schools, comparing them to other students in the same grade and school[68]. They find that future charter school students do *worse* than their peers in both reading and maths. Hoxby conducts a similar exercise in Chicago, this time comparing students' annual gains. Future charter school students' annual gains are 20% smaller in maths and 30% smaller in reading.

Finally, the data on Edison schools (a for-profit company that managed charter schools), which operate(d) in 23 states, suggests that Edison schools also experienced negative selection of students: Edison students score 12 national percentile points below other students in their districts and are 11% less likely to be judged proficient on criterion-referenced tests; moreover, for the four states for which there is longitudinal data prior to entry is available, their individual trajectories are more negative, prior to entry, than students in the public schools from which they are drawn[69]. [This is not surprising, given that Edison specialises in providing education to disadvantaged students.]

Hoxby also provides more aggregated evidence on selection and choice by race. She looks at all charter schools in operation for the 2000-01 school year, generating an odds ratio that any given student is black, Hispanic or poor, relative to the district in which the charter school is located, or relative to the public school that is physically closest. In both the district and the school comparisons, 'the odds ratio is smaller than one for white students and Asian students; substantially larger than one for black students; slightly larger than one for Hispanic students; and substantially larger than one for poor students'. Although these are of course imperfect exercises, she concludes that the evidence strongly suggests that charter schools are '*not* cream-skimming in any conventional racial, ethnic or economic way'. On the basis of this evidence it appears that charter schools are accepting disproportionately minority and poorer students.

In summary, local studies of charter school choice produce different results on the extent to which choice has been exercised by students of different race, socio-economic status, and ability. More aggregated studies of charter schools and Edison schools suggest that ethnic minorities and low-achievers are more likely to enrol in charter schools.

3. What has been the effect of charter school choice on segregation in public education?

Consistent with the more aggregated evidence on who exercises choice of charter school, a recent and influential study has suggested that racial minorities in the US are tending to segregate themselves within them[70]. The study looks at the make-up by race of charter schools in the 16 states with statewide enrolments of over 5,000 students in 2000-01. These states accounted for 94.5% of the charter school population. At the state level, charter schools enrol higher percentages of black students and lower percentages of white students relative to non-charter public schools. This pattern is essentially repeated for other minorities and at other levels of analysis. There are also pockets of white isolation, where white students are as isolated in charter schools as black students are elsewhere. The authors suggest that minority students are *isolating themselves* within charter schools, as does an earlier, smaller study .

This study addresses only the issue of segregation by race. However it makes the important point that the question of whether school choice is likely to exacerbate segregation in schools is *separate* in practice to the question of whether more advantaged families are likely to monopolise new choices. The way in which students will distribute themselves across schools under a policy of choice will therefore depend not only on issues of equity and selection, but also on social conditions more generally, and on the nature of the supply side (many

70 Frankenburg, E and Lee, C 'Charter Schools and Race: A lost Opportunity for Integrated Education' Cambridge, MA: The Civil Rights Project at Harvard University

71 Wells, A.S., Holme, J.J., Lopez, A., & Cooper, C.W. (2000). 'Charter schools and racial and social class segregation: Yet another sorting machine?' In R. Kahlenberg (Ed.), A notion at risk: Preserving education as an engine for social mobility (pp. 169-222). New York: Century Foundation Press.

72 Bettinger, E. *The Effect of Charter Schools on Charter Students and Public Schools* Occasional Paper No. 4 – National Centre for the Study of Privatization in Education 1999

73 Hoxby, C. '*School choice and school competition*: Evidence from the United States', 2003

charter schools are set up with the express purpose of catering for disadvantaged, low-achieving or minority students).

4.The effect of charter school competition on regular public schools

Studies examining the effect on public schools of competition from charter schools have been undertaken in Arizona (6.7% of pupils enrolled), Michigan (3.8%), as well as in Texas (1.1%) and North Carolina (1.4%).

An early study by Bettinger explores the effect of charter school competition on Michigan public schools[72]. As a proxy for competition from new charter schools, Bettinger uses proximity to one of ten universities where the governor appoints the board; he then relates this to public school pass rates. Bettinger finds that charter schools in Michigan attract students that have lower pre-charter scores than students in neighbouring public schools. This produces a mechanical increase in public school test scores when students leave for charter schools; however despite this, Bettinger finds a small, significant and *negative* association between competition from charter schools and relative pass rates in public schools. This is in contrast to Hoxby who, in a later study, finds that charter schools in Michigan have a positive effect on performance and productivity in public schools. In the same study she finds similar, larger, effects for Arizona.

Hoxby relates academic outcomes in Arizona and Michigan public schools to district enrolment in charter schools[73]. Controlling for a variety of factors, she finds that Michigan and Arizona public schools that faced 6% enrolment in charter schools made considerable gains each year on national tests. In both cases the improvement trends were significantly better than in the period before charter school choice was properly introduced (6% district enrolment), and significantly better than the improvements made by public schools that did not face the possibility of students leaving for charter schools.

In North Carolina, charter schools are legally independent of the school district. They can be approved by local school boards, by the state university or by the state board of education; however all cases must finally be passed by the state board. They are obliged to provide free transportation for all students living within the district, but also for those living over one and a half miles from the school. Charter schools receive 100% of district funding. In 1996 there were no charter schools in North Carolina: in 1999 there were 100; and in 2000 1% of North Carolina's public students were enrolled. In two studies, Holmes relates public school performance to a number of measures of charter school competition, generally based on distance[74]. He finds that a greater number of charter schools within a given distance is associated with better test performance in public schools. The effect wears off as distance increases.

As in a number of states, charter schools in Texas differ in their relations to school districts. 'Open enrolment' charter schools in Texas are legally separate from the district and receive their funding from the state. 100% of district per pupil funding follows students from public schools to charter schools. They must provide the transport that school districts are legally obliged to provide. In 2000 there were 200 open enrolment charter schools with approximately 47, 5999 students. Controlling for a range of possible factors, Bohte et al. relate charter schools enrolment and district charter school concentration to average pass rates and average daily attendance[75]. There is a small, but not statistically significant, association between greater enrolment and pass rates. There is a slightly negative association for the number of charter schools; however the author suggests that this is due to the fact that charter schools are in many cases more likely to set up where public school quality is poor.

In summary, in all but one study, competition from charter schools is associated with improved public school performance, although the effects are not always significant or large.

74 Holmes, G. *The Effect of Charter School Competition On Traditional School Quality*, Department of Economics, East Carolina University, 2001. Holmes et al. 'Does School Choice Increase School Quality?', Working Paper, 2003

75 Bohte et al. (2003), 'Examining the Impact of Charter Schools on Public School Performance', Paper for the National Meeting of the Midwest Political Science Association, Chicago.

In 1996 there were no charter schools in North Carolina: in 1999 there were 100; and in 2000 1% of North Carolina's public students were enrolled

---

76 Hoxby's papers
are available at:
http://post.economics.harvard.
edu/faculty/hoxby/papers.html
Hoxby emphasises consistently
in her work that studies need to
control for the possibility that
more schooling options are likely to exist where schools are
already performing poorly.
Within her work, controlling for
this possibility consistently
makes a difference to the
results.

77 For an discussion of this
see Hanushek, E.A., Kain, J.F.
and Rivkin, S.G. 'Disruption
versus Tiebout Improvement:
The Costs and Benefits of
Switching Schools', NBER
Working Paper No. 8479

The competitive effects on public schools of 'traditional' forms of school choice: private school choice and choice through the housing market

Within the school choice literature in the US there are a large number of studies investigating the effects of 'traditional' forms of school choice: choice of independent school, or choice between school districts – exercised through the housing market. These forms of choice have been around for a long time, and commentators have suggested that they might therefore shed light on the long-term effects of extended choice in the public sector[76].

More specifically, it is argued that they can tell us about the long-term effects of competition on public education. These choices are of course importantly different to extended choice in public education: because they both impose weaker incentives on public schools (because they lose funding less directly than newer forms of school choice) and larger costs on parents and pupils (because they have to pay fees, exercise choice through the housing market, and so on)[77]. For this reason we leave out the usual questions of which families have been more likely to take advantage of choice, and what has been the effect of parental choice on segregation.

In addition, it is worth emphasising that choice of school through the housing market operates differently in the US than in the UK. The influence of inter-district choice in the US is mediated by the American system of public school finance, which relies heavily on local property taxes. Most importantly, it is also worth remembering that, compared with the UK, the US has a much larger supply of low-cost private schools (85% of which are religiously affiliated): the lack of low-cost private providers of education in the UK present unique difficulties for policies designed to expand the supply side of public education. Nevertheless, it is argued that a *general* competitive effect may be apparent. If these more traditional forms of competition improve public schools despite the additional costs they impose on low-income families, then this adds weight to the argument that choice can work to improve quality across the board in public education.

Effects of competition between public and private schools

There are a number of studies in the US that assess the impact of competition from private schools on public school quality and efficiency. Caroline Hoxby has studied this issue, as part of a particularly influential programme of research into the effects of various forms of competition on US public schools. Hoxby finds that, in metropolitan areas, private school enrolment is associated consistently with better performance among public school students (including outcomes such as earnings later in life) and greater efficiency among public schools.

On the other hand, the majority of reports reach less positive conclusions. Studies at the state level have generally reported no significant association between measures of competition from private schools and public school quality. Although Couch et al. (1993) find that increased private school enrolment is associated with higher test scores in North Carolina public schools[78], Newmark (1995), who repeats the experiment and finds no significant results for twelve other specifications, suggests that the original result is not sufficiently robust[79]. At the state level, a number of other studies have also found no significant results, in Texas[80], Illinois[81] and Georgia[82]; or they have found neutral effects, for example in Washington[83]. In Florida, the association between measures of private school choice and public school quality were negative: an early study found that increased private school enrolment was associated with a decrease in public school results the following year[84]; a later study produced re-estimates of the Florida data, this time looking at the effects across high and low-income districts : for high-income districts[85] the results were ambiguous; for low-income districts they were substantial and negative.

Kang and Greene have in a recent study related the number of private schools in New York state counties, to public schools' efficiency in producing various outputs[86]. They find that competition from private schools is associated with greater efficiency in some cases; however, the effects are inconsistent and vary depending on which measure is used.

In summary, the association between various measures of private school competition and public school quality and efficiency is mixed in these studies. Although Hoxby consistently reports a positive association, the majority report indifferent results. In addition, one study reports negative effects for low-income districts.

78 Couch, J.F., Shughart, W.F. and Williams, A. 'Private school enrolment and public school performance'. *Public Choice*, 1993, 76: 301–312.

79 Newmark, C.M. 'Another look at whether private schools influence public school quality: comment, *Public Choice*, 1995, 82: 365–373.

80 Wrinkle, R.D., Stewart, J and Polinard, J.L., 'Public school quality, private schools and race', *American Journal of Political Science*, 1999, 43: 1248-1253.

81 Sander, W. 'Private schools and public school achievement', *Journal of Human Resources*, 1999, 34: 697-709.

82 Geller, C.R., Sjoquist D.L., and Walker, M.B., 'The effect of private school competition on public school performance', *NCSPE Working Paper* 2001, www.ncspe.org.

83 Simon, C.A., and Lovrich Jnr, N.P., 'Private school performance and public school performance: assessing the effects of competition upon public school student achievement in Washington State', *Policy Studies Journal*, 1996, 24: 666-675.

84 Smith, K.B. and Meier, K.J., 'Public choice in education – markets and the demand for quality education', *Political Research Quarterly*, 1995, 48: 461–478.

85 Maranto, R. Milliman, S. and Stevens, S. 'Does private school competition harm public schools? Revisiting Smith and Meier's 'The case against school choice'', *Political Research Quarterly*, 2000, 53: 177-192.

86 Kang, B-G., and Greene, K.V., 'The effects of monitoring and competition on public education outputs: a stochastic frontier approach', *Public Finance Review*, 2002, 30: 3-26.

87 Kenny, L.W. and Schmidt, A.B., "The Decline in the Number of School Districts in the U.S.: 1950–1980." *Public Choice*, April 1994, 79(1–2): 1–18.

88 Hoxby, C.M., 'Does competition among public schools benefit students and tax–payers?' *American Economic Review*, 2000, 90: 1209-1238.

89 Marlow, M.L., 'Public education supply and student performance', *Applied Economics*, 1997, 29: 617–626.

90 Husted, T.A. and Kenny, L.W., *Evidence on the impact of state government on primary and secondary education and the equity-efficiency trade-off*. Journal of Law and Economics, 2000, 43: 285–308.

Effects of choice though the housing market on public schools

The other 'traditional' form of choice that exists in the US is choice through the housing market, or 'Tiebout' choice. Because of district consolidation and changes in States' school finance arrangements, parents in the US now have less opportunity than they did to exercise Tiebout choice. Nevertheless, Tiebout choice is still the most common and the most influential form of school choice in the US[87] and a number of US studies have attempted to relate the quality or efficiency of public schools to the degree of inter-district choice available to their parents.

Hoxby finds that increased Tiebout choice is associated with raised achievement and lower spending within metropolitan areas in the US[88]. The effects are not significantly different for lower or higher income families; however there is some suggestive evidence that the effects are larger for better-off, non-minority families. Unlike private school choice, in the case of inter-district choice, these positive effects are also echoed in the majority of studies. In another cross-state study, Marlow finds that a greater number of schools and school districts are associated to some degree with higher public education spending, but also with better achievement among public school students and lower dropout rates[89]. Finally Husted and Kenny relate states' achievement in SAT to the proportion of education expenditures funded at the state level (a proxy for government – monopoly – intervention)[90]. They report mixed effects, but find in general that the monopoly measure is associated with lower test scores.

At the state-level, the majority of studies of inter-district choice also report positive associations with public school performance.

In contrast, Hanushek and Rivkin have, in an influential study, found positive associations between inter-district choice on the one hand and student achievement and teacher quality on the other. Students' value-added achievement is related to the concentration of students by district and by school across 27 'Metropolitan Statistical Areas' (MSAs) in Texas. There is little evidence of a significant relationship for the smaller MSAs. However, for the five largest MSAs the association is significant and positive. In addition, the authors relate the same measure of choice to teacher quality, measured as *variance* in teacher quality, which is itself measured in terms of the distribution of students' achievement. ['It is not that variance measures quality, rather it is the case that variance in instructional quality should decline the stronger the commitment to such quality']. They find that less competition (as measured above) is associated with *greater* variance and so, they argue, with poorer teacher quality. Finally, they find that in general the association is positive and substantial only for low-income students.

This result is in line with a large number of other studies at the state level. Tiebout choice is found to be positively associated with achievement in studies of Kentucky[91], Ohio[92], and California[93], as well as with increased allocative efficiency in Texas[94], and with greater technical efficiency in New York State[95].

In summary, the availability of choice through the housing market is associated fairly consistently with positive outcomes for the performance and the efficiency of public schools. In one case the gains were substantial only for low-achieving students. Given the absence of any studies of open enrolment policies between public schools (which are sometimes competitive), choice through the housing market is the only form of parental choice in the US to produce results for choice between regular public schools. The crucial question, given fairly positive outcomes is: what is it about choice across these administrative, legal and fiscal divides that produces effects; and to what extent can these conditions be re-produced between public schools within these boundaries?

The competitive effects on public schools of voucher policies

Effective, publicly funded voucher programmes operate in: Milwaukee, Wisconsin; Cleveland, Ohio; Florida; Vermont; Maine and Georgia. In addition, there are several private scholarship funds, the most notable being Children First America and the Children's Scholarship Fund[96]. Out of the voucher schemes, Milwaukee, Florida, Vermont, Maine and Georgia are the most relevant for our purposes, since it is only for those schemes that research has addressed the impact of choice on public schools. With the exception of Vermont and

91 Borland, M.V. and Howson, R.M., 'Students' academic achievement and the degree of market concentration in education', *Economics of Education Review*, 1992, 11: 31–39. Borland, M.V. and Howson, R.M., 'On the determination of the critical level of market concentration in education', *Economics of Education Review*, 1993, 12: 165–69.

92 Blair, J.P. and Staley, S. 'Quality competition and public schools: further evidence', *Economics of Education Review*, 1995, 14: 193–98.

93 Zanzig, B.R., 'Measuring the impact of competition in local government education markets on the cognitive achievement of students', *Economics of Education Review*, 1997, 16: 431–41. Marlow, ML. 'Spending, school structure, and public education quality. Evidence from California', *Economics of Education Review, 2000*, 19: 89–106.

94 Grosskopf, S., Hayes, K., Taylor, LL. and Weber, WL. 'Allocative inefficiency and school competition', *Proceedings of the 91st Annual Conference on Taxation*, 1999b

95 Kang, B-G. and Greene, K.V. *The effects of monitoring and competition on public education outputs: a stochastic frontier approach*, 2002.

96 See the Education Commission of the United States for details of all programmes

97 The voucher value in 2003 exceeded almost 40% of the participating schools' per pupil costs.

Maine, these states are also unusual in not allowing private schools to ask parents to pay more than the voucher amount.

Milwaukee and Florida

The vast majority of voucher schemes in the US restrict the offer of vouchers to a specific group of pupils. This is true of Milwaukee and Florida, as well as the majority of the voucher programmes not included in this review. In Milwaukee vouchers are offered only to students whose family income is at or below 175% of the federal poverty line level of income. [As a rule this means any student eligible for a free or reduced price lunch, which works out at around 185% of the poverty line level of income.] In Florida, vouchers are restricted to all students in schools that receive an 'F' two years out of four on the Florida C Assessment Test (FCAT). In Milwaukee, parents can take their voucher to private schools, including religious schools. In Florida, families eligible for a voucher can transfer to public or private schools.

Favourable studies of these targeted schemes have been particularly influential in the UK. This is not so much because advocates of choice in the UK generally favour targeted choice schemes, as because advocates have argued – some say rather ambitiously - that the positive results from these programmes demonstrate that choice schemes can be designed to benefit the worse-off, even in cases where it is made available to all service users. In this way these studies have been particularly influential for those advocating choice on left-wing grounds.

Starting in the 1990-91 school year, the Milwaukee Parental Choice Program made all public school students with family income at or below 175% of the federal poverty line eligible for vouchers, which could be used at any private, non-sectarian school willing to take students at or below the voucher amount. Total enrolment in the scheme was capped at 1% of pupils. In 1998, the Wisconsin Supreme Court upheld the program, stating that vouchers could be redeemed at religious schools and raising the total enrolment ceiling to 15%. This has been accompanied by a steady rise in the vouchers' value, from $2,446 in 1991, to $5,783 in 2002[97]. Both student and school participation in the programme rose dramatically in 1998: the number of schools participating increased more than three-fold; the number of students increased almost four-fold. In 2002 there were approximately 100 schools and 11,156 students participating in the programme[98].

The degree of voucher competition faced by Milwaukee public schools depends on the proportion of their pupils eligible for free school meals. Taking a variety of other factors into account, two sets of studies have found that a greater proportion of students on free school meals has been associated with better academic performance in Milwaukee public schools since the introduction of the voucher programme. This does not apply before the 1998 Supreme Court decision: studying the program in its early years before the program was upheld, Chakrabarti found that competition bore no significant relation to improvement; and although there were some positive shifts in schools with pupils eligible for vouchers, the school with the most pupils eligible improved the least. However Chakrabarti found a stronger association after the programme was upheld, and this conclusion is repeated in a very influential study of the Milwaukee scheme by Hoxby[99].

Milwaukee public schools are classed by Hoxby according to the number of their students eligible for a voucher. The schools 'most treated' by competition had over two thirds of students eligible for vouchers. The 'somewhat treated' schools had less than two thirds (but over 25%), and the 'untreated' schools – a control group of similar schools from an area of Wisconsin where the voucher was inapplicable - had no students eligible. 'While the improvement gains remained flat or unimpressive in the control schools between 1997 and 2002', Hoxby finds that the 'most treated' and somewhat treated' public schools generated sizeable gains on their pre-competition scores in national exams, with the largest improvements in the 'more treated' schools; this is despite their having many more pupils that were African American, Hispanic or eligible for free school meals.

Because the programme restricts choice specifically to low-income families, it could be objected that these improvements are explained largely in terms of low-income students leaving public schools[100]. For Milwaukee, Hoxby addresses this point explicitly: assuming that the scheme drew the very worst-performing pupils from Milwaukee public schools,

98 Belfield et al. 'School Choice and the Supply of Private Schooling Places: Evidence from the Milwaukee Parental Choice Program', *Occasional Paper No. 84*, National Center for the Study of Privatisation in Education, Teachers College, Columbia University, 2003

99 Chakrabarti, R. 'Can Increasing Private School Participation in a Voucher Program Affect Public School Performance?', *Evidence from the Milwaukee Voucher Experiment*, Mimeo, Cornell University, 2003. Hoxby, C. 'School choice and school competition: Evidence from the United States', 2003.

100 Ladd, F. 'Comment on Caroline M. Hoxby: School choice and school competition: Evidence from the United States', *Swedish Economic Policy Review* 2003,10: 67 - 76

In Florida any schools receiving an 'F' two out of four years on the FCAT become eligible for various kinds of corrective action

101 These answers should give us the confidence to design second-generation programs that are larger, better financed, and more ambitious in tackling issues like compensatory funding and varying vouchers with student and school characteristics'. N.B. the test for peer effect – even if we assume that vouchers took out the worst students in Wisconsin public schools, 'the departure of voucher students could not account for more than 25% of the actual improvement in Milwaukee public school achievement'.

102 Richard, A. 'Florida Sees Surge in Use of Vouchers', *Education Week*, September 2002

103 Chakrabarti takes additional p/p funding into account – low-performing schools are given priority when applying for certain grants, and the state has earmarked funds to recruit teachers to work in schools that receive D and F Grades.

104 Low-performing schools are given priority when applying for certain grants, and the state has earmarked funds to recruit teachers for schools that receive D and F grades. Unlike Greene, Chakrabarti does control for changes to per pupil funding.

105 For a detailed account of the controversies surrounding Greene's study, which includes the studies by Browne and Ladd, as well as others, see Carnoy, M. 'School Vouchers: Examining the Evidence', *Economic Policy Institute*, 2001. See Chakrabarti especially for various responses to these issues, including the stigma / finance objection.

she argues that 'the departure of voucher students could not account for more than 25% of the actual improvement in Milwaukee public school achievement'[101].

In Florida any schools receiving an 'F' two out of four years on the FCAT become eligible for various kinds of corrective action, which includes – but is not limited to – the offer of vouchers to its students for public or private schools. The vouchers are worth the lesser of per pupil spending in the public schools (currently $6,232) or the private school cost. For private schools, families can continue to use vouchers until the children reach the final grade level of the schools they are attending. In the 2002-03 year of the FCAT, 129 schools had received at least one 'F'; students in 10 schools had become eligible for vouchers since the grading of schools began in 1998. Of the 9,000 pupils eligible for vouchers in 2002, 577 have switched to private schools and 900 had gone to other public schools[102].

Greene, and also Chakrabarti, has found that 'F' schools experienced higher annual gains in achievement compared to schools that performed better on the FCAT[103]. Both authors, but particularly Chakrabarti, take into account a variety of alternative explanations, arguing that the threat of vouchers must explain a substantial proportion of the gains in achievement. This claim has proved very controversial. For Greene's study in particular, commentators have questioned the accuracy of the statistical estimates; however the central objection is that the gains may be due instead to the financial aid or to the 'stigma' associated with poor performance[104]. Critics add weight to this argument by pointing out that Browne and Ladd found similar results for schools performing poorly on the Texas and North Carolina's assessment schemes, which do not impose vouchers on their failing public schools[105].

Maine and Vermont

Although the majority of vouchers restrict choice to a sub-set
of disadvantaged pupils, Maine, Vermont and Georgia offer
voucher programmes for which all pupils are eligible. These
have been less influential than the targeted schemes. Although
there is very little information on issues of equity in uptake and
segregation, there are a number of studies relating voucher
competition to outcomes in public schools.

Since 1869 and 1873, Vermont and Maine have allowed
parents to use public funds to send their children to public or
non-sectarian private schools of their choice. These schools are
permitted to charge parents additional fees. So long as the
sending town or district pays, 'tuitioning towns' can send students anywhere within the state or even outside it. The schemes
were established primarily to meet demand for compulsory
schooling in rural areas; currently 20% of secondary students
in Vermont and 18% in Maine use the scheme. Hammons has
conducted a study of the two for the Milton and Rose D.
Friedman Foundation[106] Taking into account several factors –
in particular per-pupil funding - Hammons relates public
school test scores to the distance to all tuition towns within a
seven-mile radius. He finds that substantial gains in test scores
are associated with an increase in the competition measure.
The effect is present in less affluent areas and in rural as well
as urban areas. However the author reminds us that both
states are 95% white.

Georgia

The Georgia 'Pre-K' programme allows parents of kindergarten
children to choose between approved public schools and
private providers, including religious organisations. Parents
can cross catchment areas and district boundaries; however
schools operated by local school systems are not compelled
to take students from outside the district, although they
may do so if they wish, and if capacity permits. In 1996 the
programme served 57,000 seven year olds. In 1999 it served
60,995, which makes around 54% of the eligible population.
Providers are allowed to make a profit but are not allowed
to charge parents fees. Over half of the providers are in the
private sector.

106 Hammons, C.W., 'The
Effects of Town Tuitioning in
Vermont and Maine', Mimeo,
Milton & Rose D Friedman
Foundation, 2001, www.fried-
manfoundation.org

107 Gary, T. et al. 'Can Competition Improve Educational Outcomes?' Prepared for the National Institute for Early Education Research, 2003

Controlling for a number of different factors, Gary et al. relate competition to public school test scores, to students being held back a year, and to teachers' ratings of school readiness[107]. They find that competition is associated consistently with positive outcomes. However, the outcomes associated with private school competition are different to those associated with public school competition: private school competition is associated with improvements in grades and retention, but does not significantly affect teachers' assessments of school readiness; by contrast, competition from public schools has no significant association with grades, but is positively related to retention and school readiness.

In summary, competition from voucher schools is associated fairly consistently with improvements in public schools. The targeted schemes have generally been the most influential, and have reported large improvements. No studies report a negative association.

School choice: New Zealand[108]

The policy

New Zealand's school choice reforms were introduced with the 1989 Education Reform Act. Studies of school choice in New Zealand are potentially interesting for the UK because they report effects of choice between regular public schools. Such studies in the UK reported mixed results and the majority of studies from other countries usually address the effects of new forms of school choice such as vouchers for independent schools. One of the problems with the studies of the UK reforms was that the reforms did not go as far as some advocates deemed necessary – in terms of parental choice, its financial implications for schools and also in terms of schools' flexibility in responding to them. Research from New Zealand could therefore shed light on the potential consequences of more radical forms of choice between public schools in the UK. Unfortunately, not only is there very little research from New Zealand (see below), but it is arguable that the New Zealand parental choice reforms went less far than those in the UK.

School choice in New Zealand has, for example, been constrained by a version of the Surplus Places Rule imposed in the UK, which prevents schools from expanding effectively where spare places remain in local schools. In addition there have been other restrictions in New Zealand on parental choice, on funding and on budgetary flexibility for schools.

The original intention – certainly of the Picot Taskforce, whose recommendations informed the Act – was that compulsory education should be arranged on the choice of provider model: parents would be able to choose freely between government schools; a substantial proportion of funding would follow pupils to and from schools; and schools would have some flexibility in their use of funding, with budgets for important

108 Much of this material comes from Harrison, M. *Education Matters: Government, Markets and New Zealand Schools*, Education Forum, 2004 – a pro-market report on education reform in New Zealand.

109 In 1993 fewer than 3% of schools had opted to become bulk-funded. In 1999 – following financial incentives to do so – 31% of schools had signed up: these accounted for 40% of all students and 25% of the schools with students from low-income areas. In 2000 autonomy discretion over teachers' salaries was abolished for all schools.

110 A study of 24 primary schools between 1993 and 1997 did find that the connection between funding and enrolment could go in various directions: nearly 30% of the schools in the sample experienced a drop in enrolment over the period, but received increased operational funding from the government; 43% experienced greater enrolment and increased funding, while 15% experienced greater enrolment but received less funding [ESRA (Economic and Social Research Associates Limited),*School funding 1996-1998*, 1999, unpublished document (quoted in Harrison, M., 2004)]

111 Between 1989 and 1991 students within a school's 'home zone' were guaranteed a place at that school, while places for out of zone students were allocated by ballot. This policy then gave way to a longer period (1992 – 1999) during which *compulsory* priority for students within home zones was abolished, but school boards were allowed to determine their own enrolment scheme for over-subscribed places. All schemes had to receive final approval by the Secretary: primarily, this required schools to demonstrate that the school would be over-crowded without the scheme. In 1999 legislation was passed to try and ensure students a place at a 'reasonably convenient' school. In 2000 The Education Amendment Act again required schools to enrol in-zone students; after that extra places were allocated according to a set of priorities set out in the act; finally, remaining places were allocated by ballot. For a full account of the many changes see: LaRocque, N. and Kaye, J. Enrolment Scheme Provisions in New Zealand', Briefing Paper no. 3, Education Forum 2002

materials held at the level of the individual school. Not all of these conditions were implemented fully. There is much more controversy than usual over New Zealand on how far the reforms went in practice, and whether or not the reforms have amounted to a 'real' choice scheme, and as a result we have found no decisive answers on the practical implications of the reforms. [The more detailed evidence on these questions is summarised in the footnotes.] However it does seem plausible that they were constrained in ways that prevent New Zealand from indicating the potential effects of more radical parental choice between public schools in the UK.

Neither the costs of teachers' salaries, nor all central support services were devolved to school budgets. It was a voluntary option for schools to become 'bulk funded', in which case they would have flexibility on these issues; however 'bulk funding' was abolished in 2000, and at the height of the initiative, in 1999, only 31% of schools had signed up for a devolved budget[109]. In addition there is an unsettled disagreement within the literature on the extent to which funding followed pupils under the reforms, with one study showing the connection between enrolment and funding in primary schools going in various directions[110]. Finally, the arrangements for allocating school places were variable, and either allowed schools to produce their own admissions procedures, which were then approved by the Secretary of State for Education, or placed heavy emphasis on 'zones of right' around schools[111]. As a result, commentators have often focussed on New Zealand as a lesson on the consequences of combining school choice with admissions criteria which either leave a substantial amount of room for selection of pupils by schools, or which rely heavily on geographic criteria for allocating scarce places.

1. Did parents exercise choice?

It appears that parents did increasingly exercise choice of school following the introduction of open enrolment in 1991. From 1990 to 1991 - when students within the 'home zone' of a school were guaranteed a place and out-of-catchment places were allocated by lottery - the proportion of students not using the nearest school increased from 22% to 31%, and had risen to 35% by 1995 and it is reported that the intakes of some schools almost halved between 1990 and 1993[112]. In general it appears that schools experienced considerable volatility in all components of income in the period following the reforms[113]. This has made some schools extremely cautious over investment; however the extent to which volatility in any of these various sources of income has to do with parental choice is unclear.

2. Which parents exercised choice?

Much of the evidence relevant to this question focussed on the characteristics of the schools that tended to gain or lose pupils during the period following the reforms. For example, various commentators have reported that schools with lower socio-economic 'decile rankings' have been more likely to experience falls in enrolment than schools with higher decile rankings, which generally experienced rises in enrolment. Fiske and Ladd examine enrolment changes in the Auckland, Wellington and Christchurch areas from 1991 to 1996. They found that enrolment fell significantly in 1 – 3 decile schools (in some cases over 30%) and that enrolment rose by about 5% in 8 – 10 decile schools[114]. Similarly, Ainsworth et al. report that, in Christchurch, state schools with the lowest socio-economic decile rankings were more likely to experience declining enrolment[115]. Looking at the period 1995 to 1998, Fiske and Ladd also report that schools with a greater proportion of minorities experienced greater declines in enrolment, taking into account other factors likely to affect enrolment[116].

112 Reported in Harrison, M: *Education Matters: Government, Markets and New Zealand Schools*, Education Forum 2004

113 The Smithfield reports; Gilling, M., 'The Resourcing of New Zealand Schools', *Education International Working Papers* no 7, 2003

114 Fiske, E. and Ladd, H. *When Schools Compete: A Cautionary Tale*, Brookings Institution Press, Washington, DC, 2000

115 Ainsworth, V., Anderson T., Clements, C., Heggie, S., Rogers, R. and Martin, D. (Undated) *Tomorrow's Schools and Freedom of Choice – A Recipe for Disaster: A study of the effects of roll changes on Christchurch state schools*, Education Policy Research Unit, University of Canterbury, Christchurch, New Zealand.

116 Fiske, E. and Ladd, H. *When Schools Compete: A Cautionary Tale*, 2003

---

various commentators have reported that schools with lower socio-economic 'decile rankings' have been more likely to experience falls in enrolment than schools with higher decile rankings, which generally experienced rises in enrolment

---

117 Waslander, S and Thrupp, M Choice, 'Competition and segregation: an empirical analysis of a New Zealand secondary school market; 1990-93', *Journal of Education Policy*, 1995, vol. 10: 1, 1-26

Although the overall picture suggests some polarisation, by itself this may tell us fairly little about which parents exercised choice or about the effect of parental choice on segregation. The main burden of evidence on these questions has fallen on a (now very controversial) study conducted by Waslander and Thrupp, which looks at 11 schools over the period 1990 to 1993[117].

Waslander and Thrupp detect a fairly large increase over the period in the number of pupils attending an 'adjacent' school; that is, a school that was not their local but was nevertheless not 'distant'. The headline results come from this group of students. They find that students from low socio-economic groups on a *national measure* were more likely to choose an 'adjacent' school in the years following the reforms. On the other hand, they find that the students choosing 'adjacent schools' were generally of higher economic status as compared to individuals living within the same defined zone. They argue that the first measure is too highly aggregated, and that the second captures our concerns about equity in up-take more fully. They conclude overall that up-take of choice has been skewed towards more advantaged families.

This conclusion has generated a great deal of controversy; indeed some commentators claim that the results and the conclusion straightforwardly contradict one another. The sample is anyway small and so may not be able to withstand its current status as, effectively, *the* result for New Zealand. Ignoring this point, a natural conclusion is that both of these results are important: it is desirable, and certainly not meaningless, that open enrolment should have been followed by greater exercise of choice by lower socio-economic groups on a national measure; it would be still more desirable still if those students exercising choice were fully representative as compared to the students within the same 'zone'.

In summary, there is no decisive evidence on equity in take-up of choice by parents in New Zealand. Schools with low socio-economic decile ratings have lost pupils relative to schools higher up the socio-economic scale; however this is consistent with equity in up-take. [In the case of New Zealand, what there really is a suggestive *overall* picture, and we return to this at the end.] The only direct evidence relating to this issue is from a small-scale study. This reaches a mixed conclusion, which can be interpreted as reporting significant, but certainly not total, equity in take-up.

118 Fiske, E. and Ladd, H. *When Schools Compete: A Cautionary Tale*, Brookings Institution Press, Washington, DC, 2000

3. What was the effect of parental choice on segregation in public schools?

Using the same sample, over the same period, Waslander and Thrupp also report changes in segregation. Again, they report two sets of results, favouring the latter. In *both* cases the results jump around to such a degree that it is unclear whether there is any determinate results for either measure. First, they look at segregation between the 11 schools over the period: they find that segregation is *lower* in 1993, on a number of measures, than it was in 1990. Then, they compare segregation in the six suburb schools in the sample to segregation as it would have been had every child attended the school nearest to their home. For segregation the result is better in 1993 than it would have been had every student attended his or her local school: for segregation by parental employment, it is worse.

Fiske and Ladd rely on the results above in their discussion of socio-economic segregation; however they do look independently into the issue of race[118]. They calculate dissimilarity indices for minority and Pakeha students in urban schools over the period 1991 to 1997. They report that segregation by ethnicity rose over the period by about 1 percentage point in primary and intermediate schools and about 3 percentage points in secondary schools. With the exception of some Auckland wards, residential segregation fell during the period and so, in general, school segregation by race was higher than residential segregation. The authors therefore suggest that students' movements under the school choice reform contributed to an increase in segregation by race.

In summary, then, although considerable changes in schools' enrolments are reported over the period following the introduction of open enrolment, there is little evidence on corresponding changes in segregation. It is very unclear whether or not choice has acted to increase or decrease segregation by socio-economic status, although apparently there has been no drastic move in either direction. A more definite, small, increase is segregation by race is reported over six years of open enrolment. Overall, then, New Zealand does little to support any strong conclusions about school choice policies and segregation, although it does appear that choice (in the form it took in New Zealand over the period) has been associated with a small increase in segregation by race.

4. What was the effect of choice on educational outcomes; and how were any costs and benefits distributed?

New Zealand does not systematically collect and release information at the national level of students' achievement in exams. As a result, few commentators have attempted to establish a connection between parental choice and student achievement. Fiske and Ladd report a widening achievement gap between the best and the worst performing schools in the country's three major urban areas, as well as an increased concentration of minority and poor pupils in unsuccessful schools. Although this certainly suggests polarisation of good and bad schools over the period since the reforms, the exact relation to choice remains unclear. However this does arrive along with the evidence that schools in low-income areas have experienced enrolment and resources problems over the period since parental choice was introduced, and also with some evidence of increased segregation of pupils in poorly performing schools. It would seem reasonable, therefore, to conclude that the overall picture is suggestive of polarisation under choice, and that the results from New Zealand are at best indifferent or inconclusive.

School choice: Chile

The Policy

In 1981 Chile introduced nationally a set of school choice reforms that included both choice between public schools and also the provision of vouchers for independent schools. Existing research in English focuses almost exclusively on the effects of vouchers for independent schools. Along with the evidence from Sweden, and also most of the evidence from the US, the evidence from Chile therefore relates to choice policies that are accompanied by new forms of supply in public education. It is always different to make useful comparisons across countries, particularly in the case of Chile, whose political context is unique; however one important difference between the cases of Chile, Sweden and the US is that new 'choice' schools in Chile have been permitted to select students. Both parental interviews and admissions tests are permitted as selection procedures for admitting pupils to voucher schools in Chile.

119 Delannoy, F., 'Education Reforms in Chile', 1980-98: a lesson in pragmatism, Country Studies, Education Reform and Management Publication Series, Vol. 1, No. 1, June 2000

The original set of school choice reforms in Chile brought with them considerable autonomy for schools in managing their budgets. Responsibility for the public schools was transferred from the Ministry of Education (MOE) to roughly 300 municipalities. At the same time, the contract between the MOE and the national teachers' union was abrogated, generating increased flexibility for municipalities over pay, as well as hire and fire. However, budgetary flexibility is the one element of the reforms to have been reversed totally by the new democratic government in 1991. In 1991 laws were introduced guaranteeing teachers life tenure and centrally negotiated wages. [This was accompanied by a significant pay increase (125% in real terms between 1990 and 1998)[119]]. Currently, schools do not have control over hire, fire or wages.

120 Otherwise the new government left the structure of the reforms largely in tact: new reforms related mostly to increased funding for schools in disadvantaged areas. For an account of the changes see the above article, as well as:

121 Sapelli, C and Vial, B 'The performance of private and public schools in the Chilean voucher system' *Cuadernos de Economia*, Anos 39, No 118, pp423-454 2002

By law the mayor may give the control over their non-personnel budget, but few mayors have taken this step[120].

By contrast, the reforms designed to make funding follow the pupil to his or her chosen school have remained largely in tact. As a result of the original 1981 reforms, a large proportion of funding in Chile is determined on the basis of school enrolment (weighted by the level and type of education received by the student): it is allocated to schools every month on the basis of average attendance over the previous three. Per pupil funding in Chile is not adjusted according to the characteristics of individual pupils. However there are substantial differences in schools' budgets depending on where they are located and their inclusion in MOE programmes. Arranging municipal (public) schools into funding quintiles, Sapelli and Vial report that schools in the fifth quintile receive on average funding equivalent to an additional 71% of their pupils' vouchers[121]. As a result of such funding initiatives, and as with so many school choice reforms, there remains some disagreement on the extent to which funding really follows pupils to and from schools.

We have uncovered very little research on the choices formally and practically available to parents in Chile. This is particularly true for choice between municipal schools, as existing research in English concentrates almost exclusively on the policy of vouchers for independent schools. The policy of vouchers for independent schools allows for parents to take state per pupil funding with them to independent (voucher) schools, although the exact effect that this has on schools budgets is fairly unclear. Since 1993, such schools have been permitted to ask parents for contributions, which

---

In 1991 laws were introduced guaranteeing teachers life tenure and centrally negotiated wages. [This was accompanied by a significant pay increase (125% in real terms between 1990 and 1998)[119]]

---

are then partially offset by reductions in per pupil funding.

Voucher schools are also free to establish their own admissions and expulsion policies, which leaves a substantial amount of room for selection of desired pupils by schools. Students in Chile are not offered transport to support them in exercising new school choices.

Because there is not a great deal of research on Chile in English, and because the research we did locate generally points in the same direction, this section is fairly short. Disagreement, where it exists, relates more to methodological issues and to the extent to which results can be transferred to other settings. These considerations – we remind the reader – are excluded in this review[122].

1. Did parents exercise choice under the reforms?

Existing evidence relevant to this question focuses on parents choosing voucher schools, rather than parents choosing between municipal schools. It appears that parents have taken advantage of new school choices and that this has generated a substantive response on the supply side.

The introduction of vouchers for private schools was followed by a fairly large increase in the number of private schools, and in the proportion of students attending voucher schools[123]. More than 1,000 private schools were created from 1982 to 1985, increasing their number by about 30%. The majority of these (84% in a sample) were private, non-religious and for-profit. Enrolment has transferred over the period from public to voucher schools. Enrolment in public schools hovered around the 80% level all through the 1970's and up until the introduction of vouchers in 1981. Then it dipped rapidly, reaching the 60% level in 1990. At the same time enrolment in private schools remained fairly constant throughout the 1980's but then doubled, reaching 30% of total enrolment in 1986. The evidence suggests strongly that the effect of vouchers on enrolment was largest in urban, populated and wealthy communities[124].

2. Which parents exercised choice?

There is little direct evidence on which families have been more likely to exercise choice under the reforms. Gauri

122 Methodological controversies surrounding the Chile results arise in particular from the fact that choice was introduced simultaneously across the whole country, while there is no pre-reform data on achievement. Hoxby, C. 'School choice and school competition: Evidence from the United States', 2003, gives these and other objections to the papers summarised here. In addition the extent to which results can be transferred to other countries is likely affected by Chile's unique political context.

123 Hsieh, C and Urquiola, M. *When schools compete, how do they compete? An assessment of Chile's nationwide school voucher program*, 2002. Carnoy, M and McEwan, P. *Does Privatisation Improve Education? The Case of Chile's National Voucher Plan*, 1998

124 Hsieh, C and Urquiola, M. *When Schools Compete, how do they compete? An assessment of Chile's Nationwide School Voucher System*, 2002

125 Gauri, V. *School Choice in Chile: Two Decades of Educational Reform*, University of Pittsburgh Press, 1998

126 Parry, T. 'Will pursuit of higher quality sacrifice equal opportunity in education? An analysis of the education voucher system in Santiago', *Social Science Quarterly*, 77(4): 821 - 841

127 Hsieh, C and Urquiola, M. *When Schools Compete, how do they compete? An assessment of Chile's Nationwide School Voucher System*, 2002

conducts a survey of 726 households in the greater Santiago area. By relating parents' answers on the school attended by their children to their answers to other survey questions, he suggests that families lower down on the socio-economic and achievement scale have faced constraints on exercising choice of school[125]. He reports that students attending top schools (not schools other than the closest) were more likely: to pay more in fees; to incur greater transportation costs and to take a test; to have a mother with college, or some secondary, education; and, finally, to belong to a family with a car, greater income and greater assets.

Private schools in Chile have been permitted to select pupils, for example through testing or parental interviews. Gauri reports that the overall rate of testing in the subsidized private sector as revealed in the survey was 28%. In addition, Parry presents evidence – also from Santiago – to suggest that private schools have used both testing and interviews to select desired pupils[126].

In summary, there is little *direct* evidence relating to this question, although there is evidence on the socio-economic status of students served by voucher schools (see below). Local surveys from the Santiago area – a metropolitan area – suggest that voucher schools in Santiago have exercised their right to select desired pupils and that this is happening more in *'top'* *schools*. Students attending top schools have also been more likely to incur greater transportation costs and so it is possible that transport has acted as a constraint on low-income families exercising choice of school in Chile.

3. What was the effect of school choice on segregation in public education?

Hsieh and Urquiola suggest that the primary outcome of the introduction of voucher schools was an increase of sorting by *ability*: they argue that regular municipal schools experienced growth in the proportion of low-achievers under voucher-school choice[127]. With regards to the segregation by socio-economic status, there is also evidence that voucher schools cater for students higher up the socio-economic scale. For the 1998 distribution of enrolment by socio-economic status, Naradowski and Nores divide students into socio-economic quintiles (5 is the highest). Compared to municipal schools, voucher schools serve a greater proportion of students from the 5th (28% compared to 19%) and the 4th quintiles (48% compared to 40%). Compared to voucher schools, municipal schools serve a greater proportion of students from the 1st (75% compared to 24%) and 2nd quintiles (64% compared to 35%). Municipal schools also serve a greater proportion of students form the 3rd quintile than voucher schools (55% compared to 42.3%)[128].

In summary, evidence at the national level suggests that students with higher socio-economic status and ability are clustered to some extent in voucher schools. However it is not clear exactly why this is the case. [As above, it appears that voucher schools are more likely to set up in areas with more advantaged pupils, and so this is likely part of the explanation.] The clustering effect is strongest at the more extreme ends of the socio-economic scale.

4. What was the effect of parental choice on academic outcomes; and how were any effects distributed?

From 1991, the new government introduced a range of reforms designed to increase funding for students with lower socio-economic status; and studies have reported that, over the period, the Chilean educational system has demonstrated greater equity in the distribution of achievement by socio-economic status[129]. By contrast, studies relating achievement to measures of voucher-school choice have in general reached negative, or fairly indifferent, results.

McEwan and Carnoy relate local private school density to achievement in public schools over the early 1980's to mid 1990's[130]. They divide the results into metropolitan regions and non-metropolitan regions (they state that three-quarters of compulsory school age children live in non metropolitan regions). The metropolitan regions yield a small, positive association. Outside metropolitan areas they report a small negative association, suggesting that choice has worked differently in non-metropolitan contexts. Hsieh and Urquiola relate 1990 test scores in public schools to municipal private school enrolment: the association is significant and negative[131]. In addition they find evidence of a widening gap in educational

128 Ministry of Planning and Cooperation (1999), reported in: Naradowski, N and Nores, M *Socio-economic segregation with (without) competitive education policies. A comparative analysis of Argentina and Chile*, Documento 53, Centro de Politicas Educativas, 2001

129 See: Bravo, D., Contreras, D. and Sanhueza, C., *Educational Achievement, Inequalities and Private/Public Gap: Chile 1982-1997*, Department of Economics, Universidad de Chile, 1999

130 Hsieh, C and Urquiola, M. *When Schools Compete, how do they compete? An assessment of Chile's Nationwide School Voucher System*, 2002

131 Hsieh, C and Urquiola, M., 2002

achievement between the top and bottom socio-economic groups, and there is suggestive evidence that this effect has been strongest where choice has been most effective. They emphasise that any effect of competition has to be disentangled from the effects of sorting: they respond to this point by relating municipal private school enrolment to aggregate outcomes at the municipal level in both voucher and municipal schools. They find no significant association in almost all cases. In general the results that are not statistically significant are negative.

In summary, it appears that the various reforms introduced by the new government have contributed to greater equity in achievement overall. Some commentators have suggested that, as these were introduced alongside school choice, choice may have catalysed these improvements. However those studies that relate choice to public school performance in the period before these reforms suggest that voucher-school choice is associated with negative or indifferent results. In one study, a small, positive association was reported for metropolitan areas.

School choice: Sweden

The Policy

School choice reforms in Sweden have attracted a great deal
of international interest. Unsurprisingly, studies from Sweden
have been particularly influential for those advocating choice
on left-wing grounds. This is in part because Sweden is
associated naturally with re-distributive policies, and also
because, in contrast to the Chilean school choice reforms,
Sweden has introduced new providers that are not permitted
either to charge parents fees, or to select pupils by ability (as
with charter schools in the US). The reforms began in 1990,
with a policy of substantial decentralisation. The authority
to run primary and secondary education was devolved to the
municipalities. In addition, wage setting for teachers was also
de-centralised during the 1990's, after an agreed national pay
increase for teachers. In 1992, Sweden then passed two sets
of choice reforms: choice between public schools and choice
of independent (voucher) school. It is worth discussing
these separately; and in doing so, it is important to keep
in mind that, because education in Sweden is significantly
de-centralised, most of the key policy variables differ according
to municipality. As in Chile and the US, the majority of
evidence in English relates to choice of new schooling options.

It appears that the majority of parents in Sweden exercise
choice between regular public schools, rather than choosing
to attend voucher schools (see below); however research in
English on Sweden relates mainly to voucher-school choice.
For choice between regular public schools, arrangements
vary - as de-centralisation has meant that different municipalities
implement different policies. Municipalities vary as to whether
they allocate funding per pupil, or to the extent to which they

132 The stated principle for public school choice was that municipalities should satisfy parents' preferences subject to space limitations.

133 National Agency for Education (2003), Valfrihet och dess effekter inom skolområdet, Skolverkets rapport nr. 230.

allow schools to determine their own admissions arrangements - although, in practice, the guiding principle for allocating children to schools is distance[132]. They also differ in terms of transport arrangements, although most municipalities will not provide transport for pupils to attend public schools outside them. Finally, municipalities are free to decide how they should deal with schools losing pupils and funding.

Independent, voucher schools in Sweden receive around 85% of public, per pupil funding: the precise value of the voucher has varied with the abolition of fees for voucher schools in 1997, and with negotiations over fair compensation for municipalities' unique responsibilities. What remains unclear from the literature, however, is the extent to which regular public schools lose funding when their students transfer to voucher schools. It is likely that this varies with the policies' of different municipalities. For voucher schools, on the other hand, funding arrives and leaves with pupils.

Parents in Sweden are free to choose any independent school within the country so long as places are available. Independent schools are not in general permitted to select pupils by ability. However an important exception to this rule is Stockholm, which, since 2002, has admitted all secondary students on the basis of performance. In general, municipalities will not arrange transport for students attending a school outside them, and so availability of transport has potentially been a constraint on parents' choosing voucher schools.

1. Did parents exercise choice of voucher school?

The majority of families who choose a school other than their local choose to attend a public (state) school, rather than a voucher school. A recent survey of parents by the National Agency for Education reports that choosing a public school other than that dictated by the residence principle is twice as common as choosing a private alternative[133]. The survey also reports that around a quarter of parents stated that they chose the closest public school.

However, parents in Sweden have exercised choice of voucher school and this has produced a response on the supply side. Following the introduction of vouchers for independent schools, there has been an increase in the number of independent schools and the proportion of pupils attending. There were around 90 independent schools in 1992. By 2002 there were 539, with 5.7% of pupils attending. The post-reform growth in independent schools has been largely confined to schools with a general educational profile: prior to the reforms independent schools tended towards special pedagogical profiles, while in 2002 only 17% had a non-general profile. The growth in private schools is also largely an urban phenomenon. Between 1992 and 2001 the private school share increased from 2% to 7.7% in the most urbanised areas (areas were arranged into quartiles by population density); in the least urbanised areas it increased from 0.1% to 0.2%[134].

2. Which parents exercised choice of voucher school?
Unpublished research by Hsieh and Lindahl reported that pupils attending voucher schools in Sweden tended to be from immigrant backgrounds, and to have parents with a university education[135]. A report from the Swedish SNS Welfare Policy Group reached similar conclusions: students whose parents had received a university education were 4.5 percentage points more likely to attend voucher schools than children whose parents had a compulsory education only; foreign-born students were 3.3 percentage points more likely to attend them than native-born students of Swedish ancestry[136]. However it appears that these differences in attendance are best explained in terms of voucher schools' educational profile. Both associations – immigrant status and parental education – were reduced to statistical insignificance when considering only voucher schools with a general economic profile (83% of voucher schools in 2002).

In summary, up-take of voucher-school choice by parents has been equitable for schools with a general educational profile. It has been skewed towards specific families only for schools with a special educational profile. This demonstrates again the importance of the nature of the supply side in determining the outcomes of school choice policies.

3. What was the effect of voucher school choice on segregation?
The only direct investigation of the impact of choice on

134 Bjorklund, A et al. 'Education, Equality and Efficiency – An analysis of the Swedish school reforms during the 1990's' *Economic Policy Review*, 2004 [English translation of the 2003 report from the SNS Welfare Policy Group]

135 134 Bjorklund, A et al. 'Education, Equality and Efficiency – An analysis of the Swedish school reforms during the 1990's' *Economic Policy Review*, 2004 [English translation of the 2003 report from the SNS Welfare Policy Group]

136 134 Bjorklund, A et al. 'Education, Equality and Efficiency – An analysis of the Swedish school reforms during the 1990's' *Economic Policy Review*, 2004 [English translation of the 2003 report from the SNS Welfare Policy Group]

137 Translation of a report from the Statistical Office in Stockholm See also: Soderstrom, M and Uusitalo, R, 'School Choice and Segregation', Working paper, 2004

138 Waldo, S. *Municipalities as Educational Producers - An Efficiency Approach*, Working Paper Department of Economics, Lund University, 2000

139 Waldo, S *Efficiency in Public Education*, Working Paper, Department of Economics, Lund University, 2002

140 Sandstrom, F. and Bergstrom, F. 'School Vouchers in Practice: Competition Won't Hurt You!' Working Paper, *The Research Institute of Industrial Economics, 2002*

segregation in Sweden covers Stockholm, which in 2002 began selecting all students attending compulsory secondary schools on the basis of performance. The probability that eligible students go to a school other than the neighbourhood school has increased (in some cases because students have not been admitted to the local school on grounds of ability). At the same time segregation has increased on all estimated dimensions. Turning specifically to segregation by income, in the wake of the reform an additional 9% of students would have to change schools for there to be an equalisation of family income across schools[137].

In summary, we found little evidence on the effect of new school policies on segregation in Sweden, in particular for those schools that are not permitted to select students. Stockholm has, along with a policy of school choice, introduced selection by ability for all secondary school students. This has been associated with increased segregation on all counts.

4. What was the effect of voucher school choice on educational outcomes; and how were any costs and benefits distributed?

Again, there we have found no research that relates school performance or efficiency to the availability of choice between regular public schools. In two studies Waldo relates the municipal enrolment of private schools in general (not just voucher schools) to the productivity of public schools in Sweden. In a study covering 1998 to 2000 he finds no association[138]. In a later paper, which covers 1994 and 1995, he finds that municipal private school enrolment is positively associated with productivity in public schools[139]. It was also the most important of various investigated explanations of public school productivity.

In a much-cited study, Sandstrom and Bergstrom relate (a proxy for) municipal voucher school enrolment to the 9th grade test scores of 28,000 students in 1998[140]. They find a positive association for maths, but not for Swedish or English: 'the result holds for test results, final grades and the likelihood that students will leave schools with no failing grades'. In addition they find that competition 'does not have an adverse

effect' on the low-achieving pupils in public schools. Wibe
has criticised the study on the grounds that the results are too
sensitive to reasonable alternative specifications of the outcomes
of interest[141].

Ahlin relates municipal enrolment in voucher schools to
both achievement among public school students *and* achievement
among voucher school students in 9th grade exams[142]. She also
takes into account students' achievement in the 6th grade.
Again, she finds that municipal voucher school enrolment is
associated with achievement gains in maths, but not in English
or Swedish. Testing for differential results among low and high
achievers, she finds that there is no significant difference in the
association, although voucher school enrolment is associated
with slightly smaller gains for lower-performing students.

More recently, in their review of the Swedish education
reforms, the SNS Welfare Policy Group relate 9th grade test
scores available in 30 municipalities between 1998 and 2001 to
municipal voucher school enrolment (lagged over time)[143]. The
results in maths jump from significantly positive for test scores,
to significantly negative for final grades, and they suggest on
this basis that 'the results are simply not credible'. They then
relate municipal private school enrolment to grades across
the whole population of students – both voucher students
and students in regular public schools. In this case they find
a relatively small (smaller than Ahlin) positive association
with maths; however the association is effectively erased for
foreign-born students and children with low-educated parents.

In summary, the evidence from Sweden reports a positive
association between private school enrolment and efficiency
in public schools, although the author reaches mixed results
on this issue – indifferent in one case and positive in the other.
On the effect of *voucher* schools on public schools, no study
reports a negative association. Sweden therefore does not
provide evidence for the prediction that the introduction of
new forms of school choice would harm students in public
schools. However the (small) positive associations between
voucher school enrolment and students performance apply
only to Maths, and not to English or Swedish. In addition,
re-analysis of the data by the SNS Welfare Policy Group
produced the conclusion that the association between

141 Translated in the report, which describes the heated debate between them as 'fuelled by a non-negligible amount of ideological drive'.

142 Ahlin, A. *Does Competition Matter? Effects of a Large-Scale School Choice Reform on Student Performance*, Department of Economics, Uppsala University, 2003

143 Bjorklund, A et al. 'Education, Equality and Efficiency – An analysis of the Swedish school reforms during the 1990's' *Economic Policy Review*, 2004 [English translation of the 2003 report from the SNS Welfare Policy Group]

municipal voucher enrolment and performance of students on 9th grade Maths exams was too sensitive to be credible.

Early studies of voucher school choice in Sweden have been particularly influential because they have investigated directly the question of whether the association between voucher school choice and performance of students in exams was different for low-performing students. They reported that the effect on low-achieving public school students was not negative, and moreover that the positive association across both municipal and voucher students was slightly smaller but nevertheless still applied (for Maths). These results been questioned on re-analysis of the data. Reporting an association between municipal voucher school enrolment and the whole population of students, the welfare group found a small, positive association for Maths. However this was effectively erased for foreign-born students and for students with low-educated parents.

Although research from Sweden does not support the claim that new forms of choice will harm public school students, the results are mixed as to whether it will help them – particularly low-achieving or disadvantaged students.

Conclusions of the evidence of school choice

A number of different countries have introduced school choice policies, and there is substantial evidence on their effects (certainly as compared to patient choice policies). In general parents have been active in exercising choice of school and where new forms of provision have accompanied choice there have been substantial responses on the supply side, with growth in the number of voucher schools and students following the reforms. Take-up of choice by families has not been skewed systematically towards more advantaged parents: in most cases all families have participated in choice to some extent, and in some contexts – most notably in many US states – disadvantaged families and low-achieving students have been more likely to exercise choice. However, particularly in the UK, there have been marked differences between the socio-economic status of parents at the far ends of the activity scale. This manifests itself most seriously in low-performing schools and as a result these schools have in some cases polarised by intake.

The impacts of school choice policies have differed depending on whether or not schools have been permitted to select students. In cases where selection has been widespread – Chile being the most notorious example – it appears that choice has been skewed, that is has lead to increased segregation, and that it has harmed public schools. By contrast, in cases where selection has been less widespread, it seems that choice has been fairly universal, that its overall impact of choice has been to further integration in public education, and that it has worked to improve the quality of public schools – although generally the effects are not large. A caveat is the case of the US, where minority and disadvantaged students have exercised choice in such a way that they have segregated themselves in charter schools.

From the available evidence it appears that the degree of impact choice policies have made depended on whether they have introduced new providers or otherwise expanding the supply side. In the UK the effects of choice on integration were generally positive overall, however, up-take of choice was skewed for some families and studies of the competitive effects of choice were very mixed. In New Zealand the evidence was thin but not particularly encouraging. These were the two countries that introduced choice without simultaneously expanding the number of schools that parents might choose between (without incurring fees). On the other hand it is interesting that the operation of choice between school districts has been associated with improvements in public schools.

Looking in detail at the current picture in the UK, we have gone some way towards introducing parental choice of schools, on the 'choice of provider' model set out in the introduction to this paper. A large and increasing amount of funding has been taken away from Local Education Authorities (LEAs) and given instead to schools, which have been given greater discretion over their use of funding. A substantial proportion of recurrent funding has been per capita. At the same time parents have the right to express a preference for any school within or outside the LEA, although different LEAs have facilitated parental choice to different degrees - by adopting various methods for expressing and aggregating parental preferences, for allocating over-subscribed places, and for transport of students

In cases where selection has been widespread – Chile being the most notorious example – it appears that choice has been skewed, that is has lead to increased segregation, and that it has harmed public schools

to schools. Catchment areas and distance-based criteria have been used widely in allocating scarce places.

However, parental choice has operated along with a number of serious supply-side restrictions. Students have not been permitted to attend independent schools on state per pupil funding. And perhaps most importantly, a general policy of rationalisation of school places by LEAs has meant that state schools have not been as able as they might have been to respond to parents' preferences.

By contrast, in the US, many policies designed to alter the supply side of parental choice have been introduced. The academic literature on the impact of this is rich, particularly in relation to charter and voucher school policies.

In addition the US has produced an especially large number of studies designed to determine the effect on public schools of 'traditional' forms of school choice; that is, choice between school districts (Tiebout choice) and choice of private schools. When looking at this evidence though, it is important to note the differences from the choice of provider model we have been considering. Nevertheless, several commentators have suggested that these studies can shed some light on the long-term effects of competition on public schools (even if any effects cannot, because of structural differences, simply be 'parsed off' and applied to other school choice policies). There are a large number of relatively low-cost private schools in the US, the majority of which are religious. Tiebout choice is still the most important form of school choice in the US.

The only US policy for which issues of take-up and

segregation seem particularly interesting from the perspective of the UK is the charter school movement. For the other forms of choice we looked only at the effect on public school performance.

1. where services have offered more choice, have service users taken it up? Where choice in public services has been exercised, which people were able to exercise it effectively? Since choice of school is an inbuilt part of the UK system, the evidence does not tell us anything about the extent to which choice is embraced by British parents. In contrast, in the States, there is clear evidence that a significant number of parents take up the option of school choice when it is offered. This is also the case in New Zealand and in Sweden.

The British evidence does give us some information on who was able to exercise choice effectively. Given the inflexibility of the supply side under the system of choice introduced in UK schools, a concern here has been the extent to which advantaged families are able to monopolise new choices, either because schools will respond to choice reforms by adopting covert selection of pupils; or because of social and financial constraints on taking advantage of increased school choice. Evidence from school choice in the UK provides some support for the existence of both these dynamics.

There is some evidence to suggest that schools in London have covertly selected pupils in the period following the reforms, by ability and by race. It is not clear the extent to which this was in response to choice, or the extent to which covert selection among schools has lead to increased segregation. A number of studies report that families higher up the socio-economic scale are more likely to be active in choosing between schools. This result applied, in one way or another, when activity was measured in terms of some institutional or survey proxy, and also when activity was judged in terms of pupils actually moving between schools.

It is unlikely that this association is simply linear; and if this association is stronger for some groups and some contexts, then it is important to know which. Some of the evidence suggested that the association between activity and socio-economic status is marked only in specific circumstances

– for example for small groups of parents at the extreme ends of the activity scale, and also in non-urban areas with fewer schooling alternatives and fewer options for transport.

Turning to the US, the most relevant information on equity in take up of choice comes from studies of charter schools: this is the only US choice programme that allows all families to choose an alternative to the regular state school without incurring either fees or the cost of moving house. There are a large number of state-level studies that report mixed conclusions on these issues. More aggregated evidence, that crosses states, suggests that charter schools have a disproportionate number of minority and disadvantaged students. There is also some evidence, from the Edison schools programme and from charter school policies in a few states, that charter schools are experiencing negative selection of students by ability. This is unsurprising since both Edison schools and charter schools more generally are set up with the explicit purpose of taking on disadvantage students and schools.

2. How have any costs and benefits been distributed across services and service users? What effects have school choice policies had on the distribution of students across public schools?

For the UK, several studies report that segregation decreased in the period 1995 to 2001. The Cardiff study estimates that segregation was at its highest in 1988 and decreased annually up until 1995. Taking these results at face value, school choice has not single-handedly exacerbated segregation. However, the evidence is not clear on the extent to which choice, as it has been introduced for the school system in the UK, has determined. Overall the central factors driving segregation lie outside education policy.

Within education policy, a greater number of surplus places, as well as school closure are associated with increased integration. It is not clear whether any changes in either of these have been related to the operation of parental choice and are more likely related to on-going rationalisation of school places by LEAs. After surplus places and school closure, selective, fee-paying, voluntary-aided and grant-maintained schools are all associated with higher level of segregation. In addition, several studies have reported an association between specialist schools and segregation. It is unclear whether it is diversity itself that contributes to segregation, or whether it is the fact that these schools tend to recruit from wider catchment areas than other local schools. Finally, LEAs which rely heavily on catchment areas in allocating school places experience higher levels of segregation than LEAs which use other admissions procedures; LEAs that use some element of banding experience lower levels of segregation. The effect in either direction is about twice what they would otherwise expect, all other things being equal.

UK studies that have tried to relate segregation directly to parental choice have reached mixed conclusions. One found that schools with improved performance also experienced a reduction in their proportion of students eligible for free school meals, with poorly performing schools experiencing the reverse. Another reported that, within comprehensive rather than selective LEA's, a greater number of schools within a designated 'drive time' was associated with a decrease in the variability of ability within schools. These studies do suggest that parental choice can work towards segregation, although the effects are in each case small and so may be balanced out by other considerations.

Perhaps the most direct investigation on this particular issue is Taylor who relates polarisation by socio-economic intake of schools in eight LEAs, to the transfer of their students from primary to secondary schools in 1995[144]. He reports that schools at the top and bottom of the popularity scale did polarise to some extent by socio-economic status (on a pessimistic estimate 38% did so to some extent). This was due mainly for a minority of families at the far ends of the activity scale, and applied mainly for the bottom tier of schools. On the other hand, Taylor reports that, overall, choice led to greater integration by socio-economic status. This was particularly true for fairly attractive schools with average exam results, and in areas - generally urban areas - where it appears that parents have been most active in choosing schools.

A recent cross-state study of segregation by race in charter schools reports that minority students are isolating themselves

144 Taylor, C. *Geography of the 'New' Education Market: School Choice in England and Wales*, 2002

within charter schools. In some states white students are as isolated in charter schools as black students are in others. If sound, this study makes the important point that (under the combination of circumstances present in the US) the issue of segregation under school choice is separable in practice from the issue of white, advantaged families monopolising new choices. Research findings in New Zealand find similar results.

In general it appears that school choice does in some cases exacerbate segregation. However the effects are rarely large and in many cases the overall effect of choice is neutral, and indeed in the case of the UK slightly positive. The evidence therefore suggests that segregation may be less of a valid concern about school choice than has generally been thought and so may weigh less heavily on an overall decision about whether it should be extended in the UK.

3. Do choice schemes result in improved efficiency and/or quality? Do the benefits of efficiency outweigh any additional expenditure? How have any costs and benefits been distributed across services and service users?

For the UK, there is a general consensus that average performance in GCSE has improved over the period since choice was introduced. However there is on-going controversy over the progress of pupils at the higher and lower ends of the achievement scale: one study reports polarisation between top and bottom; another reports improvements for low-achievers and a – partly artificial - closing gap in exam scores. A controversial study of achievement in the National Attainment Tests reports substantial improvements for low-achievers, taking into account per pupil spending and class sizes. This applies particularly for the lowest-performing schools. The same was true when schools were ranked according to the wealth of the area.

Taking these later results at face value, it appears that choice has not interrupted, or has assisted, a trend towards greater equity in exam performance. But any isolated contribution of choice to achievement remains unclear: studies relating various (density-based) measures of choice to exam performance have reported, respectively, a negative, an indifferent and a positive association. In no case was the association large.

Turning to the US, studies attempting to relate private

school competition (generally measured as the percentage private school enrolment in a given area) to achievement or efficiency in public schools have reached mixed conclusions. These studies do not generally suggest explanations, but a plausible interpretation is that the selective and fee-paying nature of these schools (although they are less so than in other countries) has the effect of draining public schools of their better students. For most studies there is no significant association; one found a negative association for disadvantaged students in public schools. By contrast, studies relating various measures of Tiebout choice to public school achievement or efficiency consistently report a positive association. In a series of influential articles, Hoxby reports a positive association both for private school and Tiebout choice with public school performance and efficiency. In these she stresses the importance of controlling for simultaneous determination between public school quality on the one hand and the availability of alternatives on the other.

There are a number of publicly funded voucher programmes in the US that allow students to attend private schools, which are then forbidden from them charging fees. These tend to be fairly small in scale, and to rely heavily on religious schools. With the exception of Vermont and Maine they all restrict choice to a sub-set of pupils who are disadvantaged either financially or academically. Studies of these programmes have generally reported positive and substantial associations between various measures of competition from voucher schools and public school performance. The Milwaukee study has been particularly influential and suggested particularly large gains for worse-off students. On this basis commentators have argued that choice for all parents can be designed to benefit poor families.

Commentators have objected to studies of Florida and Milwaukee on the grounds that something other than choice may have brought about improvements in public schools: in Florida this is the accountability system by which schools become eligible for vouchers; in Milwaukee it is the fact that choice was restricted to the kinds of students whose exit from public schools may well have helped them to achieve better results. Hoxby states that the most pessimistic estimate leaves a maximum 25% of the public school improvements to be explained in terms of disadvantaged students leaving.

Looking at the US, studies examining the effect of charter school competition on public schools have been undertaken for Arizona (enrolment 6.7%), Michigan (3.8%), Texas (1.1%) and North Carolina (1.4%). Although enrolment and regulation vary substantially for these states, all of these states are at least comparatively willing to allow competition between charter and regular public schools. Bettinger reports the only negative association - for Michigan public schools - which is significant but small. Otherwise all studies report a positive association, including an influential study of Michigan by Hoxby. In Sweden, there was limited evidence of a positive impact of new schools on the quality of public schools.

In sum, school choice does – under the right conditions – work to improve the quality of public schools: there is significant evidence of the general 'levelling-up' effect predicted by advocates; in some cases (again, given the right conditions) this benefits have been distributed to low-achieving and disadvantaged students; there is very little evidence that these groups are positively harmed. Similar results apply for the efficiency of public schools.

It is not yet clear whether the additional costs associated with maintaining a system of school choice – in particular one which is equitable and where new forms of supply are introduce – will outweigh efficiency benefits. Barring targeted voucher schemes in the states few reported effects are substantial, but longer term and consistent effects are reported and so certainly there is little reason to suppose that costs will obviously outweigh benefits.

Patient Choice

Summary of findings

- The UK patient choice pilots have been unique in ensuring substantial take-up of choice by patients. These offer patients unlikely to be treated within 6 months the choice to be treated earlier at an alternative provider. 67% of patients in the London pilot, 75% of patients in the Manchester scheme and 50% of patients in the national cardiac scheme took up the choice offered them.

- There is also suggestive evidence that take-up has been equitable: preliminary analysis of the London pilots reveals no correlation between the deprivation index of the PCT and the take-up of choice by patients.

- Although high take-up may in part be down to the fact that these patients have had to wait six months before being offered choice, the package of support co-ordinated and provided by Patient Care Advisors has doubtless had a substantial effect. Survey evidence suggests that PCAs have been very popular with patients; in addition patients more favourable about their PCA were more likely to express satisfaction with the whole experience of choice, and, importantly, were more likely to take up choice in the first place.

- High take-up for the UK choice pilots is in contrast to low take-up for patient choice policies in other countries. Where the issue of equity in take-up has been investigated, choice has been skewed towards younger patients with higher socio-economic status. System design seems to be relevant here.

- Patients received little support in exercising choice: for example, there is little or no subsidised transport for patients exercising choice. In addition, financial incentives have been variable and unclear, and have often landed at the municipal level. Providers have therefore had little financial incentive to accept choice patients. Doubtless also, some patients have been satisfied with nearby provision: a substantial proportion exercised new choices to attend a nearer provider. On the other hand many of these patients will have been offered choice after a substantial wait.

- Some evidence suggests that GP fundholders were not particularly effective as agents of choice for patients because their incentives as contractors overcame their incentives as agents of patient choice. This raises questions for patient choice, since when choice is introduced nationally patients will often make choices through their GP. However, GP's offering choice will not face the same budgetary incentives as fundholders and will not have to negotiate on price with secondary providers. However the balance between patient choice on the one hand and PCT commissioning practices and priorities on the other is as yet an unresolved issue in policy documents.

- The impact of choice on waiting times has so far been positive in the UK.

- Taking other factors into account, the introduction of choice in the London Pilot reduced waiting times across a range of elective procedures. In addition, waiting time reductions for the London pilot have been *distributed* as advocates of extended choice predict: both those patients who did and those who did not exercise choice have benefited under the scheme.

- GP fundholders were also able to reduce waiting times relative to non-fundholders. This only applied when they themselves purchased treatment for their patients, which was generally on a case by case, by results, basis. The evidence suggests that fundholders accomplished this both by moving patients (and accompanying funding) around the system, but also through the threat of doing so.

- Fundholding status also catalysed internal market GPs' general successes in encouraging consultants to visit practices and

---

Patients received little support in exercising choice: for example, there is little or no subsidised transport for patients exercising choice.

---

attend outreach clinics, which was popular with patients. Although the overall merits of these changes are debated, this is preliminary evidence in favour of the view that choice can encourage greater *responsiveness* from providers of secondary care.

- On the balance of the evidence, the transaction costs associated with GP fundholding outweighed benefits in terms of efficiency. Whether this will be the result of current proposals will depend in part on the transaction costs associated with the fixed tariff system.

- There is almost no evidence to suggest that choice has been associated with increased selection by providers, although overall there is little evidence at all. Analysts predicted extensive cream skimming among fundholding practices; however the general consensus within the literature is that fundholders did not go in for cream skimming despite a financial incentive to do so. Apparently, policies that reduced the financial impact on fundholders of costly patients came together with inherent constraints on selection (including, but not limited to, professional ethics) to ensure that selection was not a factor.

Patient choice: the UK

145 Harrison, M *Implementing Change in Health Systems: market reforms in the United Kingdom, Sweden and the Netherlands* (2004), SAGE Publications

146 Of course, many commentators have expressed doubts as to whether these contracts really merited the name (Harrison (2004)).

There are two potential sources of evidence on patient choice from the UK:

- evidence from the internal market

- evidence emerging from the recent patient choice pilots.

These are addressed in turn.

Experience from the Internal Market: GP fundholding

The relevance of the internal market reforms

The internal market reforms are often said to have been the boldest of market-based reforms in public health care[145]. They have also been attached firmly to the issue of patient choice: greater choice, convenience and empowerment for patients were explicit aims in 'Working for Patients'; and commentary on recent choice reforms – particularly the critical commentary – has sometimes drawn on an analogy between the two. In short, evidence from the internal market could relate both to issues of patient choice and to issues of competition between secondary providers.

However it is necessary to isolate the relevant features of the internal market. There is an important difference between a system in which providers compete for funding that follows individual patients' choices, and one in which providers compete for contracts from purchasing agencies. The majority of purchasing in the internal market fell under the latter model, with health authorities agreeing large-scale block contracts with providers on behalf of a large constituency of people[146]. While such purchasing is relevant in the sense that its effectiveness is *compared* – explicitly or implicitly - in the literature with GPs contracting on behalf of individual patients, it is not itself the subject of this paper, and so we do not address it directly[147]. For this reason we address only the evidence concerning GP fundholding (see below).

A further, important, difference between the internal market and current proposals, which applies across the whole of the quasi-market – including the GP fundholding experiment (see below) – is that the internal market was designed to introduce competition on price as well as quality. By contrast, the current policy is that competition on price should in general be kept to a minimum; and the funding that follows patients' *choices* in the NHS will instead be determined according to a system of fixed national tariffs[148]. Pending the results of this (specific) fixed tariff system, we should therefore be cautious in carrying over any results from the internal market reforms.

The GP Fundholding experiment

GP fundholding was a voluntary scheme that ran between 1991 and 1999. Self-selected practices (or groups of practices) were given a budget with which they were expected to purchase a designated range of services for the patients on their lists. The scheme developed fairly spontaneously, and so arrangements would vary – according to the range of services purchased, and the number of GPs coming together into a group. However fundholders' purchasing responsibilities would often include a sub-set of elective, secondary procedures.

Whenever fundholders referred a patient for a procedure that fell within their purchasing range, they would contract with the provider themselves – instead of relying on the health authority to do so on their behalf. In contrast to health authority contracts, payment would be linked firmly to activity (hospitals did not get paid unless an adequate discharge letter was received by the GP) and contracting was often on a case-by-case basis[149]. In addition, most GPs had a fairly wide choice of provider – there was some choice even in rural areas – and so, at least in theory, fundholders were able both to offer their patients *choice*, and also to exercise a threat of exit over secondary providers.

On this basis GP fundholding bears some analogy with proposals to have funding following patients' choices at the

147 For information and evidence on the whole range of purchasing arrangements in the internal market, see: Le Grand, J et al. *Learning from the NHS Internal Market.* (1988) London: Kings Fund

148 'Reforming NHS Financial Flows: introducing payment by results'. DOH 2002. 'In adopting a standard price tariff, we are recognising that price competition is generally ineffective for hospital services.'

149 Glennerster, H 'Competition and quality in health care: The UK experience', *International Journal for Quality in Health Care,* 1998, Volume 10

150 Dixon, J 'Will practice make perfect?' *Public Finance, September 10 – 16 2004*

151 Coulter, A, Response to SMF Scoping Paper Choice: The Evidence during consultation period, September 2004

152 For a summary of the evidence, see: Goodwin, N GP fundholding. In Le Grand, J et al. *Learning from the NHS Internal Market.* (1998) London: Kings Fund And also: Le Grand, J. *Motivation, Agency and Public Policy: of Knights and Knaves, Pawns and Queens.* Oxford; Oxford University Press, 2003

point of GP referral: the experiment could perhaps shed light on the potential for GPs to act as agents of choice and exit for patients, and on the effects of patient exit and choice on the quality of secondary care. The relevance of the fundholding experiment will also be greater to the extent that the Labour government attempts to re-instate aspects of the fundholding experiment, which is apparently happening[150]. However, at present, the full extent of the analogy between GP fundholding and patient choice is not yet clear. Indeed, one of authors of a leading study on GP fundholding suggested that no-one actually thought of fundholding as a means of enabling patient choice at the time[151], but rather as a way of introducing cost-efficiency. This may help explain some of the design anomalies of the fundholding scheme which renders it somewhat incompatible with schemes more explicitly designed to enable patient choice. For example, transaction costs of GP fundholding will have depended to some extent the fact that GPs had to contract for services themselves, and that they had to do so on price. More generally, GP fundholders faced a unique set of budgetary incentives, which may or may not apply under patent choice at the point of GP referral.

Crucially, fundholding GPs were allowed to keep any surplus on their budget at the level of the practice (or fundholding group). They therefore faced budgetary incentives to do a number of things, one of which was to negotiate on price. They may also have been motivated in part by the budgetary incentive to attract patients; or, at least, certain classes of patient, as they were funded predominately per capita (adjusted for age and sex). The evidence suggests that fundholders did respond to financial incentives, although there is disagreement on whether, overall, the effect of budget holding was negative or positive, particularly from the perspective of the health service as a whole[152].

From the perspective of this review, the aim is to isolate the effects of GP fundholding most relevant to issues of patient choice, while keeping in mind that fundholders' budgetary incentives, and their circumstances more generally, will have had some impact on these as well as other outcomes. With this in mind, we now present the evidence from fundholding relevant to our three questions on patient choice:

1. did patients exercise choice?

2. which patients exercised choice?

3. what was the effect on the quality and efficiency of secondary care?

1. Did patients exercise choice as offered by GP Fundholders?
It appears that the process of health authority contracting
at a district level did a lot to restrict the choice of providers
that internal market GPs could offer their patients. Before the
introduction of contracting, GPs were free (in theory) to refer
their patients to any secondary provider; afterwards, GPs not
actually purchasing a service themselves would have to refer
patients to a hospital contracted by the health authority[153].
Exceptions could be made if a GP wanted to refer a patient
to a hospital not contracted with the district, but the process
was time-consuming and very costly[154].

Health authorities themselves were much less likely to
switch contracts than GP fundholders for fear of de-stabilising
providers, and so GPs not actually purchasing services for
themselves had relatively few options in terms of moving
patients around the system. Correspondingly, studies have
suggested that fundholders were more active in switching
referrals than the health authorities (and the GP practices that
relied on the health authorities to contract for them)[155]. While
this is significant, however, the extent to which fundholders did
so in order to facilitate patients' preferences remains unclear.

Did fundholders purchasing services themselves do much
by way of offering patients choice? This question is complicated
by the fact that fundholders had to contract for services and
negotiate prices themselves, which, along with their budgetary
concerns, may have got in their way of offering choice to
patients. In a small and early study of cataract surgery, Fotaki
found that four out of five London providers had an exclusive
relationship with one provider. The fundholders argued that
this was based on their assessment of quality and price.

An influential survey by Mahon et al. found that, although
fundholding GPs reported greater willingness to take patients'
preferences into account and to refer patients greater distance
for elective surgery, as well as a lower likelihood of considering

153 Harrison, M *Implementing Change in Health Systems: market reforms in the United Kingdom, Sweden and the Netherlands* (2004), SAGE Publications)

154 Ghodse B. 'Extra-contractual referrals: safety valve or administrative paper chase?' *Br Med J* 1995; 310: 1573-1576

155 Le Grand, J et al. (1998) Glennerster et al *Implementing GP Fundholding: wild card or winning hand?* Milton Keynes: open University Press (1994)

156 Mahon, A et al. 'Choice of hospital for elective surgery referrals: GPs and Patients' views'. In Robinson, R and Le Grand, J, Eds. Evaluating the NHS reforms (1994), London, King's Fund

157 Kind, P et al. *Evaluating the Fundholding Initiative: the views of patients.* York: Centre for Health Economics (1993)

158 Roland, M and Coulter A (eds) *Hospital Referrals*, Oxford: Oxford University Press, 1992

159 Stirling, A et al. 'Deprivation, psychological distress, and consultation length in general practice'. *Br J Gen Pract 2001; 51(467):* 456-60. This and other evidence can be found in: Dixon, A et al. 'Is the NHS Equitable?' A review of the Evidence (2003), LSE Health and Care Discussion Paper Number 11

only one hospital for elective referral, the patients of those GPs expressed a lack of willing to travel longer distances, and most expressed indifference to the issue of choice[156]. Similarly, another survey found that most patients expressed a preference to use their local hospital[157]. Coulter et al., on the other hand, found no evidence to suggest GP fundholders were consulting their patients about their referral options to any greater extent than non-fundholders[158].

In summary, it does appear that GPs purchasing services for themselves were more likely to move patients around the system. However, the extent to which fundholders worked as agents of patient choice is very unclear. Overall the evidence suggests low take-up of choice by patients, low instances of GP-Patient consultation regarding GP's purchasing decisions, and survey evidence shows that some patients expressed indifference to the issue of choice in any case.

2. Which patients were more likely to exercise choice through GP fundholders?

A central objection to GP fundholding was that it benefited some (more advantaged) patients over others. However, this was generally on the grounds that not all GPs were fundholders: much of the evidence on equity relates to this point, and to the distribution of fundholding practices across more deprived areas. Since the current plan is to extent choice to patients though all GPs, the relevance of this point is qualified somewhat. On the other hand it does raise the question of the extent to which GPs will be equally effective in offering patients choice, and how these GPs will be distributed across the country. In addition, as there is some evidence to suggest that GPs can spend less time on patients with lower socio-economic status (although these patients tend to visit primary care more often)[159], there is a question of how this will pan out in terms of differential benefits from choice offered by any given GP for patients of different socio-economic status. There are arguments in different directions on this point, but we do not address this issue here. These issues relate to the structure of primary care, which is not covered in this review.

Evidence from the internal market relating to equity in take-of choice under GP fundholding is scarce. The only issue discussed in any detail is the question of whether fundholders selected desirable patients for their lists. Fundholders had both the opportunity and the budgetary incentives to select less costly patients, and many analysts predicted extensive cream skimming by fundholding practices. This was particularly so given that fundholders were thought not to be large enough to accommodate the risk of attracting more expensive patients. However, the general view 'in the more sophisticated literature' on fundholding is that fundholders did not go in for selection, despite the incentive to do so[160]. There are various explanations as to why this should have been the case. Some have to do with policies designed to minimise the impact on fundholders of more costly patients. Others relate to natural barriers to selection of patients by fundholders.

First, fundholders could rely on a stop-loss insurance scheme: the health authorities were responsible for any individual case over £5,000 pounds in a year, although this would not have protected them against multiple admissions below this level, or from an unexpected rise in the demand for care. Second, the costs of treatment covered by fundholders tended to be relatively cheap and formula funding took into account age and gender-driven differences in cost[161]. Third, it is suggested that, although fundholder's decisions could certainly be mediated by budgetary concerns, they were – for whatever reason – consistently motivated to act in the interest of the patients closest to them, if not in the interest of the health service as a whole[162]. Finally, it is possible that fundholders did not always have sufficient information so select patients.

In summary, there is very little evidence on equity in up-take of choice under GP fundholding. It appears that fundholders did not go in for selection of less costly patients, despite the fact that existing policies would not have entirely erased their incentive to do so. It is suggested that these policies came together with natural barriers, in terms of motivation and information, to ensure that selection of patients by fundholders was not a significant factor[163].

3. What was the effect of GP fundholding on the quality or the efficiency of secondary care; and how were any costs or benefits distributed?

160 Goodwin, N 'GP fundholding'. In Le Grand, J et al. Learning from the NHS Internal Market. London: Kings Fund 1998

161 Glennerster, H. 'Alternatives to Fundholding'. International Journal of Health Services 1998; 28 (1); 47-66

162 Le Grand, J. Motivation, Agency and Public Policy: of Knights and Knaves, Pawns and Queens. Oxford; Oxford University Press, 200

163 Le Grand, J. Motivation, Agency and Public Policy: of Knights and Knaves, Pawns and Queens. Oxford; Oxford University Press, 200

164 Glennerster, H. 'Alternatives to Fundholding'. *International Journal of Health Services* 1998; 28 (1); 47-66

165 Glennerster, H. 'Alternatives to Fundholding'. *International Journal of Health Services* 1998; 28 (1); 47-66

166 Glennerster, H. 'Alternatives to Fundholding'. *International Journal of Health Services* 1998; 28 (1); 47-66

167 Baeza J, Calnan M. 'Implementing quality: a study of adoption of quality standards in the contracting process in a general practice multi-fund'. *J Health Serv Res Pol* 1997; 2: 203-211

168 Glennerster, H. 'Alternatives to Fundholding'. *International Journal of Health Services* 1998; 28 (1); 47-66

169 Audit Commission *What the Doctor ordered: A Study of General Practice Fundholders in England and Wales* London, HMSO, 1996

170 It used data from only one hospital over one year; it made no distinction between patients waiting on the routine list and other classes of patient; finally it calculated average waiting times for fundholding and non-fundholding practices according to status at the time of operation, so people who spent a long time on the list before practices changed status would still add to the practice's average waiting time. Dowling found his own results were virtually erased given these assumptions.

The evidence is that fundholding GPs did use purchasing to lever improvements in secondary care relative to non-fundholders (who relied on the health authorities to purchase services for them). However the direct evidence on quality per se is very limited. At any rate, the aim of the European quasi-market agenda, and especially in the case of the UK, was not primarily to improve quality in the narrow sense but to 'sustain quality while containing costs and improving convenience and consumer concerns of other kinds'[164]. Waiting times were a primary concern, and the most rigorous studies concern waiting times.

The main burden of evidence on quality derives from a series of observational case studies and interviews with GP fundholders, usually taken before and after they entered the scheme. 'Most of the examples concern organisational issues and convenience rather than clinical standards, but these were important to patients and most research suggested there was some real movement on these issues'[165]. Surveys of fundholders' contracts also found that they were more sophisticated and stringent on quality issues than health authority contracts[166], however a study of one multi-fund found that this was not effective in changing consultants' clinical practice[167]. Finally, the evidence suggests that fundholding status catalysed internal market GPs' relative (but not unique) successes in persuading consultants to visit practices and hold outpatient clinics. 'This proved popular with patients and meant that more attended their appointments'[168]. As a result it could be considered an example of greater responsiveness brought about through the possibility of exit.

The most extensive and rigorous research is on the question of whether GPs were able to use purchasing to secure shorter waiting times than GPs relying on the health authority to purchase for them. An early survey by the Audit Commission found that, although seasonal variations could exist between patients of fundholding and non-fundholding GPs, these variations were ironed out over the year and overall waits were usually similar[169]. However Dowling reports serious methodological flaws in the survey[170]. Dowling himself used a database survey of over 57, 000 patients to compare the waiting times for fundholder and non-fundholder patients at four providers between 1992 and 1996. He found that 'patients of fundholding practices had significantly shorter waiting times than those of non-fundholders for all four providers and over all four years', and the 'waiting times did not fall until the year that the practices joined the fundholding scheme'. An analysis of the budgets and resources available to the two groups of GPs showed they were virtually the same. Finally hospitals involved provided the same range of operations covered by the scheme to both classes of patient, and in similar case mixes[171].

Propper et al reached a similar, more nuanced result[172]. Using a data-set of 100,000 hospital admissions they found that doctors who paid for their patients' care were able to secure reductions in waiting times of about 8% compared to doctors who did not. Sometimes they achieved this by actually contracting with another provider (which they did most intensively when they entered the scheme). At other times it appears as if the threat of exit was enough to bring about improvements. Interestingly, when they were only able to choose - but not to pay for - their patients' care, fundholders and non-fundholders alike were unable to reduce waiting times for their patients.

At first sight, these results suggest that internal market GPs were able to use the exit option to the advantage of their patients, and this would seem to speak in favour of allowing funding to follow patients' choices at the point of GP referral. However their successes might be explained by other advantages rather than greater choice of providers. There are two classes of complaint here: first, that GPs that chose to enter the scheme were already the best or most privileged practices; second, that GPs who did enter the scheme were given extra resources, in the form of extra funding but also extra time and support – extra computers for example[173].

The consensus in the literature reviews we studied is that GP fundholders were not systematically over-funded[174]. [There is some truth in the claim that they were given extra time and 'soft' resources.] However the first allegation – that they were better or more privileged before they entered the scheme – remains. One respect in which this is generally agreed is that fundholders did tend to be located in affluent areas, where the patients were easier and less costly to treat. And most commentators are willing to admit that fundholders may

171 'Potential biases do not affect results of waiting time study', Dowling, letter to BMJ, *BMJ* 1998; 317: 79 (4 July)].

172 Propper, C et al. 'Waiting Times for Hospital Admissions: the impact of GP Fundholding' (2000), CMPO Working Paper Series

173 Goodwin (1998) Baines DL, Whynes DK. 'Selection bias in general practice fundholding'. *Health Econom* 1996; 5: 129-140

174 Goodwin (1998) Baines DL, Whynes DK. 'Selection bias in general practice fundholding'. *Health Econom* 1996; 5: 129-140

175 Le Grand, J. and Dixon, A. *Choice and Equity in the National Health Service*, 2004.

176 DOH Website, June 2004

Using a data-set of 100,000 hospital admissions they found that doctors who paid for their patients' care were able to secure reductions in waiting times of about 8% compared to doctors who did not

have had better contact or relations with providers before they entered the scheme. This would dilute results to the extent that studies did not control for pre-existing differences between fundholders. Many did, however, especially those relating to waiting times.

In summary, there is evidence to suggest that fundholding GPs were able to use purchasing on behalf of their patients to lever some improvements in secondary care. This is particularly true for the issue of waiting times. In addition, it appears that (or at least the evidence is *consistent* with the claim that) fundholders were able to secure waiting time improvements both by moving patients around the system, but also and by using the threat of exit. Finally, it appears that fundholders were *especially*, but not uniquely, successful in encouraging consultants to conduct out-reach programmes. There is the possibility of bias here, but this may be considered an example of exit as a means to greater responsiveness in secondary care.

The NHS Choice Pilots [175]

There are now at least nine pilots in England offering patients choice of an alternative provider for elective surgery [176]. Existing evaluation centres on three. The first – the London Patient Choice Pilot – began in 2002. Patients set to wait more than six months for an operation at their 'originating trust' were offered the choice to have an earlier operation at an alternative hospital. The scheme began covering ophthalmology, but now includes ENT (Ear, Nose and Throat) general surgery and orthopaedics, oral surgery, gynaecology, urology, plastic surgery and some neuro-surgery. The second choice pilot is a national scheme that began in 2002, covering all patients waiting more than six months for cardiac surgery. A third pilot began in the Greater Manchester area in 2003 and covers patients approaching six months on the waiting list in general surgery, orthopaedic and ENT.

Following the pilots, choice will soon be rolled out nationally: by summer 2004 all patients waiting six months or more for elective surgery will be offered a choice of provider (Phase 1); by December 2005 all patients eligible for elective surgery will be offered a choice of at least 5 providers at the point of GP referral. Under phase 2 funding will follow patients' choices, with Trusts gaining or losing at the full tariff for the relevant procedure. At present the London pilot is the only pilot to have produced evidence relating to the financial incentives associated with patient choice

1. Have patients exercised new choices under the pilot schemes?

In contrast with international experience of patient choice policies – where take-up has generally been low (see below) – preliminary data from the London and CHD schemes shows that a relatively large proportion of patients are taking up the choice offered to them: 67% of patients in the London pilot have taken up the choice to be treated at an alternative hospital; 50% have done so in the national CHD pilot; 75% have done so in the Manchester Pilot.

There are various possible explanations for why take up has been relatively high. Obviously, patients in these pilots will already have waited six months and may by then have grown pessimistic about local provision; however it is worth noting that international policies tying choice explicitly to waiting times have also experienced low take-up. In addition take-up is higher for the London scheme (as well as the Manchester scheme – 75%), and this may in part be because travel and accessible alternatives are less of a problem in these larger cities[177].

A further, likely, explanation is that patients in the UK schemes have been more willing to take up the offer of choice as a result of the support they have received in choosing. In both the London and the CHD schemes patients are contacted at around the four or five month period by a Patient Care

177 Le Grand, J. and Dixon, A. (2004) On the question of accessible alternatives currently available across the UK, see: Damiani, M, Dixon, J. and Propper, C. (2003) Mapping choice in the NHS: analysis of routine data. Kings Fund: unpublished paper.

178 Le Maistre, N et al. (2003) *Patient Evaluation of CHD choice Scheme* Oxford: Picker Institute.

179 DOH Website, June 2004

180 Le Grand, J. and Dixon, A. *Choice and Equity in the National Health Service*, 2004.

Advisor (PCA), who explains the available choices to patients and offers them advice as well as assistance, particularly with transport and accommodation for companions. Transport was free of charge for all patients, although – for the CHD scheme at least – survey evidence suggests that quite a few patients organised transport for themselves[178]. [When the scheme is rolled out nationally transport will only be free for patients covered under the existing Hospital Transport Scheme[179].] It seems reasonable to assume that the PCA 'package' as a whole will have exerted upwards pressure on take-up. Weight is added to this argument by survey evidence from the CHD scheme showing a significant relationship between patients' take-up of choice and a positive assessment of their PCA.

The Picker Institute recently conducted a survey of the patients who were deemed eligible for the scheme. 3,341 patients returned completed forms – a response rate of 79%. There was no difference in the response rate between patients who took up the offer of choice and those that did not. We should of course be aware of the problems associated with opinion surveys, in particular that patients' retrospective statements may be influenced by the choices they have made. Nevertheless, it is significant that there was a close relation between whether or not patients took up choice in the first place and their evaluation of their PCA. 61% of patients who travelled to an alternative hospital rated their PCA as 'excellent', compared to 37% of patients who remained on the waiting list. This pattern was also mirrored in their responses to other questions – whether the PCA gave enough information or made it easy to involve friends and family, and whether they kept in touch about treatment.

In summary, the NHS pilots have been unique in securing substantial take-up of choice by patients. Survey evidence supports the intuitive view that the package of support offered by the PCA has exerted upwards pressure on take-up of choice by patients. However it is not clear *which* elements of this package have been most effective, and for which patients[180]. A survey of (stated) preferences from the London choice pilot suggests that take-up of choice by patients is sensitive to a number of factors, such as the reputation of the 'choice' hospital (see below).

2. Which patients have exercised choice?

Evidence relevant to this question comes from the CHD choice scheme and the London Patient Choice Pilot.

The CHD scheme

For the CHD scheme, there is almost no information on the kinds of CHD patients that took up the choice offered them. In particular there is no data on the relative socio-economic status of the patients who did or did not take up – or who were or were not offered – the choice to receive earlier treatment at an alternative provider. However the CHD scheme has demonstrated unexplained variation in the proportion of patients deemed clinically eligible for choice in the first place and this is potentially a problem.

At around four or five months, if no definite invitation 'to come in' has been given for the patient, a clinical assessment is then made as to whether the patient is eligible to be offered an alternative provider. If deemed eligible, patients are then contacted by the PCA. Clinical eligibility rates varied substantially between trusts in the CHD scheme – from 60% to 90% – and the variation cannot fully be explained in terms of case mix. 'This suggests either that there is no professional consensus on clinical thresholds for 'moving' a patient or indeed that professionals have used this as a means of excluding their patients from the scheme'[181]. While there is currently no evidence to suggest a correlation between patients' individual characteristics and access to the CHD scheme, clearly this is an issue that deserves closer examination. It is of course possible that the variation is not related to patients' characteristics; however the variation is itself a concern, since it raises the worry that patients are being excluded or included arbitrarily.

The London Patient Choice Pilot

67% of eligible patients took up the offer to be treated earlier at an alternative provider in the London pilot. On the issue of factors affecting uptake by patients, the only information to have surfaced so far is that preliminary analysis of the data by PCT showed no significant relationship between the deprivation index of the PCT and the take-up of choice[182], although an unpublished evaluation of the LPCP has found that, whilst

181 Le Grand, J. and Dixon, A. *Choice and Equity in the National Health Service*, 2004.

182 Le Grand, J. and Dixon, A. *Choice and Equity in the National Health Service*, 2004.

183 Coulter, A, le Maistre N and Henderson L, (2004) *Patients' Experience of Choosing Where to Undergo Surgical Treatment*, Picker Institute

184 Burge, P et al. 'Do Patients always prefer shorter waiting times? A discrete choice analysis of patients' stated preferences in the London Patient Choice Project (LPCP)', *Applied Economics and Health Policy 2004:3*

take-up rates are not significantly skewed by social class, educational or ethnic background, patients in paid employment were more likely to choose an alternative hospital[183]. Given the lack of definitive evidence to indicate to what extent socio-economic factors influence the take-up of choice in this context, the findings of Burge et al. prove a useful indicator. They used survey responses from 1813 respondents to model patients preferences regarding choice options[184]. The study includes estimates of the weight patients place on various factors, such as the relative reputation of the 'choice' hospital: these weights are understood in terms of the length of the wait that patients would be willing to avoid by switching hospital, ceteris paribus. Overall, 30% of respondents stated that they would stay at the home hospital under all circumstances; 5% stated that they would switch to the choice option under all circumstances; 55% switched between the options depending on circumstances.

For all patients, survey responses implied that both additional travel and payment of travel costs reduced their willingness to choose another option in order to reduce waiting times. For the case of additional travel distances, patients' survey responses implied that each additional hour of travel time added 2.2 months to the waiting time that they would be willing to avoid by exercising choice. Payment of travel costs was associated with an additional 5.2 months wait (although this includes hospitals abroad). In addition, patients were less willing to switch hospitals in order to reduce their wait if this required them to organise (not pay for) transport for themselves.

Patients' survey responses also implied that their willingness to switch in order to reduce waiting times was dependent on the location of follow-up care: in general they were less willing to exercise choice if this involved receiving follow-up care at the chosen hospital, rather than their regular hospital. On average, patients would be willing to wait an additional 2 months if this meant that they could receive follow-up care at their regular hospital rather than at the chosen hospital. [For Ear, Nose and Throat (ENT), the implied value in terms of waiting times was 4.3 months.] Finally, patients' responses implied that they placed considerable value on feeling that the alternative hospital offered them under the LCPC had an adequate reputation: patients' responses implied that they were significantly less likely to report a willingness to choose an alternative with shorter waiting times when it was stipulated that the alternative had a worse or *unknown* reputation as compared to their regular hospital.

In order to project *equity* in up-take of choice, Burge et al. also relate patients' survey responses to their personal characteristics. They report that patients who are older, female, have low education levels, or are parents or guardians of an under 18-year old were all less likely to accept faster treatment at an alternative hospital. At the same time, different socio-economic groups (defined according to fairly extreme income categories) also placed different weights on the relative reputation of the 'choice' hospital: patients with household income over £10,000 pa placed a negative valuation on the choice hospitals having a worse reputation than their regular hospital that was over a third higher than the negative value placed on such a hospital by a patient with annual household income below £10,000.

3. What was the effect of patient choice on the quality or the efficiency of secondary care?

The London pilot is the first to produce a study related to the financial incentives associated with choice. Focusing specifically on the issue of waiting times, Dawson et al. report that the choice under the pilot is associated with reduced waiting times. In addition, they relate patients' choices in orthopaedics, ophthalmology and general surgery to (a) the behaviour of receiving hospitals and (b) to the performance of sending hospitals[185]. For receiving hospitals they find that reduced waiting times for choice patients are not associated with any expense to other patients at the receiving hospital. For sending hospitals they find that loss of patients (and funding) is positively associated with improved performance on waiting times.

In summary, there is little conclusive evidence on equity in take-up of choices by patients in the pilots, although a survey of stated preferences raises concerns. The scheme has been associated with reductions in waiting times, which have applied also for patients *not* exercising choice.

185 Dawson, D et al. 'Is patient choice an effective mechanism to reduce waiting times?' *Applied Economics and Health Policy* 2004:3

Patient choice:
the international evidence

Overview

186 Goddard, M. and C. Hobden (2003). *Patient Choice: A Review*. Report to the Department of Health. York, Centre for Health Economics, University of York.

Many public and tax-funded health systems have had a great deal of experience in offering patients choice of provider, both in primary and secondary care. Unfortunately there is very little available evidence in English - the most interesting evidence in fact comes from the UK. Many studies offer only a broad characterisation of the policy, and in many cases it is difficult even to identify from the evidence the choices available and how they are managed, let alone their larger effects.

In countries such as France, Germany, Belgium and Australia some form of patient choice has for a long time been the norm; but these countries tend not to collect information on the effects of choice for that reason[186]. Other countries have introduced choice explicitly into the system, usually as part of waiting time initiatives. However it is rare for all of the components of a competitive patient choice policy to come together in these countries – particularly because different local governments tend to implement choice differently, and to different degrees, and where they come together they have done so too recently for us to be able to assess their effects.

Given the lack of evidence, it is helpful to start with a statement of what the evidence does not tell us. The evidence does not tell us in any great detail about how public health providers respond to competition for patients: the only evidence on efficiency in general concerns the impact of choice on waiting times, and this tends to be thin. Instead evidence is limited to information on the proportion of patients taking up choice, the organisational responses of providers under patient choice policies, suggestive evidence on the impact of choice on waiting times, and finally some evidence on the characteristics of patients exercising choice[187]. Because the evidence is thin, we have decided not to present it in the usual format.

Countries where choice has been implicit

In countries such as France, Germany, Belgium and Australia, some form or other of patient choice has been assumed. However choice is not always competitive in these countries, and funding does not always follow the patient. It is not clear, therefore, that these countries should fall within the scope of this review.

Le Grand points out that studies of equity at the macro level suggest that countries with a long experience of patient choice, such as France and Germany, have not thereby incurred serious costs in equity[188]. However, the significance of this is unclear. There is evidence to suggest, for example, that take-up of choice, in France at least, is low (see below). This is perhaps related to the fact these countries do not systematically provide transport for patients making choices. In addition, as Le Grand also points out, macro studies can mask substantive inequity at the micro, or service level[189]. Studies at the micro level do suggest that take-up of choice is skewed in some of these contexts.

In a general review of the literature on several countries, Porell and Adams reached the conclusion that older patients (especially those from rural areas), pregnant women and patients with lower socio-economic status – measured in a variety of ways – are all less likely to travel further for care[190]. Studies of take-up of choice in France reach similar conclusions. Take-up in France is anyway apparently low: a study of inter-region patient movement conducted in 1997 found that only 6% of hospital stays took place outside the region of residence, and that these tended to be for more complex or technically advanced procedures[191]. There is also some evidence to suggest that patients choosing a more distant hospital tend to be more highly educated and of higher social class.

In summary, there is evidence suggesting that take-up of choice by patients in France has been low, and has been skewed by education and social class. More general evidence suggests that take-up has been skewed towards younger patients (especially in rural

187 A difficulty in this area is that micro studies of access to health care generally relate to the use of user charges rather than choice. In some countries exercising choice brings with it additional charges and in these cases it is 'difficult to disaggregate differences in access arising from choice per se and those arising from the differential costs of exercising choice'. None of the choices studied below are associated with additional user charges, although in Sweden for example a small user charge is imposed on every patient – choice or no choice. [Le Grand, J and Dixon, A (2004)

188 Le Grand, J. and Dixon, A. *Choice and Equity in the National Health Service*, 2004.

189 For a review of the literature on the NHS see: Dixon, A et al. (2003)

190 Porell, F and Adams, E (1995) 'Hospital choice models: a review and assessment of their utility for *Medical Care Research and Review* 52 (2)

191 Reported in: Goddard, M. and C. Hobden (2003). *Patient Choice: A Review*. Report to the Department of Health. York, Centre for Health Economics, University of York.

areas) and towards patients higher up the socio-economic scale.

Countries where patient choice has more recently been introduced

Several countries have introduced patient choice more recently and more explicitly, usually as an effort to reduce waiting times. In general these policies have not been accompanied with the provision of transport for patients, at least when they intend to choose a provider outside of the municipality. In addition the financial incentives accompanying choice have for the most part been both weak and variable. Municipalities have introduced incentives in different ways and to different degrees. In many cases funding will follow the patient, but only at the level of the municipality, rather than at the level of the individual provider. This gives providers little financial incentive to attract patients. The financial incentives for patient choice policies have recently been sharpened in most of these countries; however, where a more competitive patient choice policy has resulted, it has done so too recently for there to be any evidence on its effects. We present such evidence as there is by country. Again, we have not adopted the usual format due to a lack of evidence.

Denmark

Denmark perhaps provides the most extensive experience with the introduction of patient choice policies, which has taken place in several stages. Patients in Denmark have for a long time had choice of public hospitals within the county; however county hospitals' budgets remained fixed, giving them little incentive to accept patients choosing to go there, and there is no evidence that we could find on the impact on efficiency or equity of this form of choice.

At a local level, a choice arrangement existed between three counties from 1992 to 1999. These counties offered their patients a free – cross-county - choice of public hospital, with originating counties paying for treatment. It appears that the some patients did exercise choice. However the most likely motivation was to travel less far to hospital. A study attributed 39% of cross-border activity to the 12% of citizens who lived closer to a specialist hospital in the neighbouring county than to the nearest provider within their own. Such patients were more than three times as likely to exercise cross-county choice of hospital than others[192].

More recently, a number of policies have been implemented within Denmark to try and extend both choice and accompanying incentives. A national choice programme was introduced in 1993 and was strengthened until 2002, when it was replaced by a more radical choice policy tied explicitly to waiting times. Patients have been offered little support in making choices: all patients have to pay transport costs if they choose to be treated in another county, and for substantial periods GPs and patients had little information, in particular on waiting times (although this has since changed)[193]. In addition the government made it clear from the beginning that counties would not receive extra funding with which to implement choice. Finally, hospitals have had weak incentives to attract patients: incentives have varied from county to county and with national policy; where they have been strongest they have tended to fall at the county rather than the hospital level.

The 1993 'free choice' scheme offered patients a choice of public or approved private provider, so long as the provider was at the level of specification determined by the referring GP. The policy in its original form was quite restricted. Payments across county lines were kept at a deliberately low level (a flat rate based on the average marginal cost): this was designed explicitly to reduce the incentive for counties to build up capacity to attract patients from neighbouring counties. In addition counties could refuse patients if their own were waiting more than three months. Finally, counties could decide whether or not to keep payment at the hospital or the county level, which made for considerable variation in hospitals' incentives to attract patients. In fact many kept payment at the county level only.

Perhaps unsurprisingly, only a small proportion of patients exercised choice under the scheme, which led to several adjustments in 2001, including a sharpening of the incentive structure for providers. Only 2% of non-acute admissions in 1993, and 2.1% in 1996, were handled under the scheme[194]. Later on in 1999 a Ministry of Health assessment estimated that 2 – 3% of patients a year were exercising their right to choose an alternative surgical provider: most patients continued

192 Goddard, M. and C. Hobden (2003). *Patient Choice: A Review*. Report to the Department of Health. York, Centre for Health Economics, University of York.

193 An Ministry of Health website was eventually set up to show the wait to see a specialist following referral, as well as the wait between seeing the specialist and receiving in-patient treatment.

194 Goddard, M. and C. Hobden (2003). *Patient Choice: A Review*. Report to the Department of Health. York, Centre for Health Economics, University of York.

195 Hurst, J and Siciliani, L *Tackling excessive waiting times for elective surgery: a comparison of policies in twelve OECD countries* (2003) OECD

196 Hurst, J and Siciliani, L *Tackling excessive waiting times for elective surgery: a comparison of policies in twelve OECD countries* (2003) OECD

197 Goddard, M. and C. Hobden (2003). *Patient Choice: A Review.* Report to the Department of Health. York, Centre for Health Economics, University of York.

198 Vrangbaek, K and Bech, M (2001) *Organisational responses to the introduction of DRG rates for 'extended choice' hospital patients in Denmark.* Paper presented at the 22nd Nordic Health Economists' Study Group Meeting, 24-25 August 2001.

to choose their nearest hospital for treatment[195]. At the same time, the aggregate mean in-patient waiting time actually increased between 1993 and 1998, from 93 days to 110 days – reducing to 103 days in 2001[196]. There were other waiting time initiatives in place at the same time; and it is difficult to tell what would have happened in the absence of choice. Nevertheless, commentators suggest that choice, as it was introduced originally, did not have a substantial impact on waiting times in Denmark.

Because of the low take-up the scheme in the first few years, there was a renewed discussion of the framework legislation, and one of the resulting decisions was to strengthen the competitive element by introducing DRG (Diagnosis Related Groups) rates for payment. From 2000 onwards payments would reflect the national average cost for each DRG, rather than the average marginal cost as before. This produced variable incentives depending on where counties and hospitals stood in relation to the national average. However this increased the level of payment significantly and in many cases the DRG rate was higher than the fixed rate used to compensate providers within the county.

Commentators suggest that this has worked to stimulate counties' attention to the flow of patients in and out of the county. The scheme is too recent for there to be clear evidence on the impact of increased payments on waiting times or on take-up of choice, although Jensen and Jinnerup report that choice is exercised mainly by individuals living near county borders (but these patients did not necessarily seek out a nearer provider)[197].

Initial research from Vrangbaek and Bech, looking at the *organisational* impacts of the scheme for the year 2001, suggests that, in general, counties were tending to use case-based re-imbursement more frequently, and more intensively, when patients move between counties rather than within them[198]. Otherwise they found variation in all aspects of the incentive structure - the general impression being that counties took a somewhat cautious strategy on incentives. In some cases adjusting them during the budget year if overall expenditure control was threatened. They suggest that counties felt that they had more important priorities than patient choice.

Surveys of county meetings suggest that they were also worried about the impact that patient choice might have on their ability to plan and deliver services.

The following year, in 2002, Denmark introduced the 'extended' choice scheme, which accords more closely with a competitive model of a choice scheme. This scheme is linked explicitly to waiting times and embraces a wider range of providers: patients waiting over two months have the right to seek treatment at any public or private hospital in Denmark, or in an overseas contracted hospital. It is also possible that incentives will be sharpened further, as the government has experimented with activity-based payment direct to hospitals when distributing an additional subsidy to the hospital system in 2002. There is little evidence as yet on the outcomes of the renewed choice scheme, although it has been suggested that few private providers have been able to offer care at the public DRG rate.

In summary, Denmark has introduced various patient choice reforms. Until recently, these have been characterised by weak and variable incentives for providers. In addition patients have received little support in making choices. There is no evidence as yet on the effects of the strengthened scheme. The original scheme, which was accompanied by weak incentives for providers to attract patients and little overall financial support, experienced low up-take of choice by patients and no corresponding reduction in waiting times.

Sweden

Sweden also has some experience with introducing patient choice. A form of choice tied to waiting times was introduced nationally in 1991, and was abandoned in 1996. Choice was introduced again in 1997 and 1999 - in primary care and the outpatient sector. Finally all county councils have, since 2002, offered free choice of providers both within and between counties. As in Denmark, incentives for individual providers have for the most part been weak and variable. Waiting lists and times are monitored and published in Sweden (in some cases the information is very elaborate). However they are not generally presented to patients by a GP: primary care has traditionally been weak in Sweden, and patients tend to access secondary care directly. In addition transport is not provided to patients exercising choice.

It appears that Sweden does not evaluate patterns of patient choice, and so such evidence as there is concerns the organisational impacts of the schemes, along with evidence on waiting times.

The 1991 Maximum Waiting Time guarantee offered patients waiting more than three months on their local list treatment at a hospital in an alternative health 'department' or county council, or at a private provider. The scheme applied to 12 surgical procedures. In contrast to the case of Denmark, extra resources (US $70 million) were set aside in the first year; this was in addition to local support, which was to carry on throughout the scheme. However, as in Denmark, different county councils managed transfers of funding in different ways, so that there were not consistently clear incentives for hospitals to attract patients. In some cases payment landed with hospitals themselves; in other cases 'departments' were affected; finally payments were on many occasions kept at the county level.

Manning and Spanberg suggest that, although the scheme did bring about changes in providers' behaviour in relation to waiting lists, the impact of the choice element was weak. This was particularly likely to be the case, they argue, because many patients were unaware of the choices available to them – particularly at the beginning of the scheme. Only one fifth of the physicians surveyed estimated that a majority of patients knew about the guarantee and their right to choose an alternative provider, although this situation did improve over time. Despite some short-term successes, it appears that the scheme had no long-term impact on waiting times: by 1993 waiting times had begun to increase again; by 1996 they reached the same level as when the guarantee was introduced. The scheme was abandoned in 1996.

Since then, Sweden has taken a new approach. In addition to some extensions of choice in primary care and the outpatient sector in 1997 and 1999, all county councils have since 2002 introduced free choice among public providers within and between counties. The scheme covers primary care, outpatient specialist and elective inpatient care. Again, the financial arrangements are varied. Patients may not choose an alternative provider above the original level of specialisation. Moreover, originating counties must provide explicit approval before care is provided. As yet there is no evidence on the impact of the scheme[199].

In summary, there is little evidence from Sweden on patient choice. The evidence is thinner, but suggests that Sweden has had a similar experience with patient choice as Denmark; that is, that take-up of choice has been low and that there has been no corresponding decrease in waiting times.

Norway and the Netherlands

The Netherlands has for some time offered patients a choice between approved public hospitals. Options have further expanded through various waiting time initiatives, which have also offered financial incentives based on DRG payment direct to hospitals. There is little information on outcomes.

A maximum waiting time initiative existed in some form or other in Norway between 1990 and 2000, offering patients a choice outside the county. Hospitals failing to treat patients in time have not always been penalised financially. This is despite the fact that Norway has been uniquely successful in introducing DRG-based payment in to public healthcare. This also remained the case after guidelines were introduced in 1997 requiring counties to arrange treatment elsewhere for patients in a serious condition, who were not treated within 3 months. This guarantee was abandoned in 2000 and replaced by a right to 'necessary care' which prioritises patients with greater clinical need. In 2001 the Act for Patients' Rights ensures for patients a choice of public or approved private hospital at the original level of specialisation. There is no evidence as yet on the success of these schemes.

199 For an up-beat, but opaquely sourced, account of the success of patient choice in reducing waiting times in Stockholm, see: Hjertqvist, J. *The health care revolution in Stockholm: http://www.fcpp. org/publication_detail.php?Pu bID=441*

Patient choice: conclusions

Have patients exercised choice?

The national Coronary Heart Disease (CHD) choice pilot and the London Patient Choice Pilot (LPCP) are the only pilots to have produced any substantive evidence as yet. The CHD pilot and the LPCP are unique in reporting a substantial proportion of patients taking up the option to be treated elsewhere: 50% of patients in the CHD scheme took up the choice offered them, along with 65% in the London pilot. [75% for took up the offer in a Manchester pilot]. By contrast, patient choice policies in other countries have invariably experienced a low proportion of patients taking up the offer of an alternative secondary provider. Because patients in the pilots have been offered choice only after a substantial wait, it is of course possible that they have taken up choice out of desperation with local provision. On the other hand, it is plausible that the package of support offered through the PCAs has also exerted up-wards pressure on take-up; and a retrospective survey of the CHD scheme supports this view, showing a positive association between patients' overall assessment of their PCA and whether or not they took up choice in the first place.

It is significant that only a small proportion of patients have taken up the offer of an alternative provider in other countries – even where choice has been attached to maximum waiting time guarantees, and has been offered through a GP. It is plausible that in many cases this reflects a genuine preference for local provision: in several cases patients have used new choices to attend a nearer hospital in another county. On the other hand, low take-up could relate also to common features of these policies. In their earlier stages, these policies have offered hospitals weak and variable incentives to attract patients that have generally landed at the municipal, rather than the administrative, level. [The financial incentives accompanying choice have since been sharpened, usually alongside an extension of choice; however this has happened too recently to determine any effects.] In addition, patients have not always been aware of available choices or have received little substantive support in exercising them.

GP fundholders were more able than health authorities to switch patients between hospitals and also reported greater willingness to facilitate patients' choices. However there is little evidence that they were effective as agents of patient choice. Surveys of fundholders' patients suggested that many were indifferent to the issue of choice. In addition, an early, small-scale study suggested that fundholders' contracting activities may have got in the way of offering patients choice.

There is lower take-up for the CHD scheme than for the Manchester and London pilots. Otherwise we have found no *evidence* from any of the sources that take-up for patient choice is lower in rural areas.

Which patients have taken up choice?

Studies of patient choice in other countries have reported that active take-up of choice by patients has been skewed towards younger patients and patients further up the socio-economic scale. This may be related to low levels of support for patients in making choices. There is no evidence from the GP fundholding experiment on this issue, except that fundholders apparently did not go in for selection even though financial compensation did not rule out the incentive to do so.

Preliminary evidence by PCT from the London NHS pilot shows no significant association between take-up of choice and the deprivation index of the PCT or the socio-economic, educational or ethnic background of the patient. However, greater availability of transport and available alternatives in London may be a factor, and initial unpublished results have more recently discovered a correlation between being in paid employment and choosing to attend another hospital. Furthermore, survey answers from the London pilot (summarised also above) implied that patients who were older, female, had lower education levels or were parents or guardians of an under-18 year-old were all less likely to accept faster

200 Coulter, A, le Maistre N and Henderson L, (2004) *Patients' Experience of Choosing Where to Undergo Surgical Treatment*, Picker Institute

GP fundholders were more able than health authorities to switch patients between hospitals and also reported greater willingness to facilitate patients' choices

treatment at an alternative hospital. In addition, they implied that different socio-economic groups (defined fairly drastically) placed different weights on the relative reputation of the alternative hospital: the implied negative valuation placed on the alternative hospital having a worse reputation was almost a third higher for patients with household income over £10,000pa.

A further cause for concern relates to the process by which patients are deemed clinically eligible for choice. Clinical eligibility rates in the CHD scheme varied between trusts from 60% to 90% and this cannot be explained fully in terms of case mix. This suggests 'either that there is no professional consensus on clinical thresholds for 'moving' a patient or indeed that professionals have used this as a means for excluding their patients from the scheme'. Similarly, reviews of the LPC scheme found that two thirds of technically eligible patients had not, in the event, been offered choice. It was deemed likely that this was due to deliberate obstruction on the part of the providers, with the eligibility rates varying between the five originating trusts from 14% to 42%. The risk of provider obstruction will be similarly significant when choice moves to the point of referral (the GP). Initial investigations seem to indicate GPs are not enthusiastic about this project or the prospect of having to involve their patients more fully in their referral decisions. The possibility of having to introduce an incentive or sanction procedure to ensure GPs' full cooperation with the scheme is being countered[200].

What has been the effect of patient choice on efficiency / quality and how have these been distributed?
There has been no sustained reduction in waiting times

associated with patient choice policies in other countries, which have anyway experienced low take-up.

Taking other factors into account, fundholding GPs were able to reduce waiting times for their patients relative to non-fundholders. At the same time, fundholders were unable to reduce waiting times for those procedures that they relied on the health authorities to purchase for them. The evidence is consistent with their reducing waiting times by actively moving patients around the system and also with their doing so through the threat of moving patients to an alternative provider.

The evidence also suggests that fundholders were especially, but not uniquely, successful in encouraging consultants to hold outreach clinics. The merits of this are debated, but it proved popular with patients. The fundholding experiment therefore provides suggestive evidence for the claim that a threat of sending patients (and the associated funding) elsewhere can work to improve some aspects of the quality and the responsiveness of secondary care. The transaction costs associated with fundholding most likely outweighed any benefits in terms of efficiency.

The London pilot is unique in reporting results relating to the financial incentives associated with patient choice. The scheme has been associated with some reduction in waiting times. Crucially, these have applied for those patients who did exercise choice and moved hospitals, as well as those who remained at their local hospital (either through an active choice to do so, and also through not exercising choice and remaining where they were). The existing evidence does therefore *not* support the claim that choice will distort clinical priorities at the expense of non-choice patients and instead gives some support to the view that choice can bring about some improvements for patients not exercising choice.

General policy implications

The cases of choice in health and education are very different, and so for the most part we discuss them separately. Some general conclusions are given below.

1. The various outcomes of choice schemes covered in this review, including those relating to equity as well as efficiency, all relate closely to the way in which they are designed. This is not to say that choice policies can (or have been) designed to produce infallibly any desired conjunction of outcomes; neither does it imply that nothing can be said about choice which is both general and useful. However it is clear from the evidence surveyed here that the question of design is fundamentally important in practice. Arrangements governing funding, selection of recipients by providers, support for recipients in making choices and the design of the supply side have consistently made a difference to the efficiency and the equity of the final outcomes.

2. This *does* imply that the debate about extending choice in British health and education should be careful of excessive generality and theory: the issue is which design features are required in order to produce desired outcomes in the UK and whether these conditions are practicable within the UK. Available alternatives to choice should be judged against the specific model of choice that emerges from this question.

3. The basic rationale behind the model of choice discussed here is that service users' choices should have tangible consequences for public services, and the most basic mediator should be the funding that follows recipients around the system. For this to be possible in practice, three features are important: (a) service

users should indeed be free to exercise choice; (b) funding should follow their choices to an appropriate administrative level; and (c), providers should have a degree of freedom with which to respond to choice. Schemes that do not meet these requirements are unlikely to bring any of the benefits imputed to them.

4. The evidence is much more limited for health than it is for education. Nevertheless, the evidence collected on choice so far suggests that competitive choice schemes can be designed to bring about some improvements in terms of quality and efficiency. Crucially, studies report fairly consistently that these benefits have been *distributed* as advocates of choice policies would predict; that is, that they apply for public providers, and that benefits have applied both for those recipients that actually exercise choice and for those that do not. This depends crucially on the detail of the design. This point applies to a more limited extent to the issue equity in up-take of choice by recipients.

5. There is no conclusive evidence on whether the overall costs associated with choice, for example additional transaction costs, work to outweigh gains in efficiency. This is not an issue which has been directly investigated in the studies considered.

6. An important issue for the debate on choice in the UK is how it can be applied to rural and non-urban areas. There is evidence in the case of education to suggest that take-up of choice in the UK has been lower in rural or non-urban areas, and also that it is more *skewed* towards advantaged service users in these areas; in addition, benefits in terms of quality and efficiency have often been significantly stronger in urban and metropolitan areas. A review of the literature on patient choice in various countries suggested that up-take of choice was more skewed towards young people in rural areas, but otherwise we have uncovered no evidence on this question for the case of patient choice.

7. Another important issue is whether or not choice policies can be made effective without introducing extra capacity or new forms of provision. There is some evidence that effective

choice is possible without new forms of provision, both for choice in education and in health. However many effective policies have involved new forms of supply. Choice has also been effective without introducing extra capacity; however as yet it is unclear whether or not choice will be effective given *current* levels of capacity. [See the individual sections for more detail.]

School choice: what are the policy implications?

Introduction

The evidence suggests that, given specific policy conditions, school choice can create a 'levelling-up effect' on the performance and the efficiency of state schools. Gains are not always large, but they are consistently distributed as advocates of schools choice would predict; that is, choice is associated with benefits for state schools, including those that are left by pupils in favour of others. The specific policy conditions required to deliver these benefits appear to include a supply side characterised by some flexibility and excess capacity, an absence of overt or covert selection of pupils and the three efficiency related criteria discussed above.

Studies investigating the impact of choice policies on low-achieving or disadvantaged pupils have reported various results, none of which are negative and some of which are positive. Assuming these same specific policy details, the evidence therefore does not support the 'pernicious' view of school choice: that it leads systematically to polarisation between best and worst; and this is especially true given that most of the policies examined have not exercised all of the available options for weighting choice towards disadvantaged students.

This does of course leave the 'deflationary' view of school choice policies: that, while they are not pernicious, nevertheless their benefits are unlikely to outweigh their costs, and so effort would be better spent on other issues. Various studies have reported efficiency gains associated with school choice, some of which have been substantial and have increased year on year. On the other hand, studies rarely consider the wider costs of implementing and sustaining effective and equitable school choice. Because very little of the research on choice conducted to date has examined this issue, there is little that can be said about this here.

Selection and cross-boundary competition

There are two general patterns in the evidence on school choice. First, to the extent that school choice policies have been accompanied by overt selection by schools then the beneficial effects of those policies have either been heavily muted or actually reversed. Second, with the exception of inter-district choice in the US, it was only those (non-selective) policies that have introduced new forms of provision into public education that consistently reported positive associations between choice and the performance of state schools. The first result is straight-forward to understand: combining choice with overt selection increases both the means and the motive for schools to select favoured pupils; the impact on overall performance is at best indifferent and the underlying distribution of benefits is inequitable. The second result, however, requires further interpretation.

Non-selective forms of school choice consistently associated with improvements in state schools are those that exist across institutional divides: that is, between regular state schools and new forms of provision in public education, and, in the US, between school districts. There are two intuitive, and compatible, lines of explanation for this. These may be the only cases in which there is sufficient capacity and flexibility on the supply side, or where the terms of competition for state schools are sufficiently competitive. At the same time the necessary variation between schools, in terms of culture, management, methods and so on may only exist across these divides.

Who chooses?

School choice policies invite two worries that both fall under the general heading: 'who chooses?' Some critics emphasise the social and financial constraints on exercising effective school choice, while also associating choice with schools choosing students rather than students choosing schools. They argue that both would act as significant sources of segregation and inequality under a system of extended school choice.

Turning first to the exercise of school choice, the evidence suggests that activity in choosing schools does tend to be skewed towards more advantaged families. This impacts most on families at the extreme ends of the socio-economic scale and those in non-urban areas, with fewer options for transport and fewer available alternatives - in these cases, availability of transport has been an important issue. On the basis of the evidence we therefore recommend that support should be provided for parents in exercising school choice, but that it should targeted towards these specific families and contexts. We will investigate this point as part of our on-going work on supporting choice.

We have encountered a general view that a policy of choice in education is inseparable from a policy allowing schools discretion over their admissions policies. The international evidence demonstrates that this is false. Moreover it gives good reason to believe that extending choice alongside selection of students by schools is likely to have negative consequences on all counts (see below for the consequences of selection for UK segregation). We therefore recommend that any extension of school choice should be in the context of minimal selection of pupils by schools.

Covert selection, on the other hand, is a complex issue. There is evidence to suggest both that covert selection operates in the UK and that some schools have responded to choice by covertly selecting desirable students. On the other hand there is evidence to suggest that selection has not been an effective barrier for low-achieving and disadvantaged students entering new schooling options in the US and in Sweden. It is likely that covert selection is arising in the UK because capacity constraints overall, and lack of flexibility within the system allows a popular school to choose its pupils. In general, policy options for discouraging selection include: regulation of providers and attention to the kinds of providers available, as well as weighted incentives for disadvantaged students (although it is important to note than commentators are not all equally optimistic about the impact of weighted funding on selection).

Choice and segregation
A final consideration is the impact of parental choice on segregation of pupils – by socio-economic status, by ability, by race,

and so on. One argument against extending parental choice in the UK is that it might add up to less integrated public education than either the status quo or some other option, such as increased use of banding criteria. An important point is that the question of whether or not this is the case is separable in practice from the question of whether or not choices are monopolised by more advantaged families, or whether schools deliberately select more advantaged pupils. This is made clear by the experience of charter schools in the US, which are usually introduced with the explicit purpose of catering to the more disadvantaged groups, and where minority and disadvantaged students have often segregated themselves.

The example of charter schools raises an important point about priorities. Segregation in this case produced higher educational outcomes for the most disadvantaged. While segregation may raise issues of concern relating to community cohesion and citizenship, it may not necessarily produce poorer educational outcomes. There may be a trade off to be made between the two values.

There is another sense in which concerns about segregation should be dissociated from education systems. The dominant causes of segregation in UK state schools lie outside education policy: on one estimate, 90% of the variation in segregation in state schools can be explained in terms of external factors. The same study reports that, within education policy, school number, school type and LEA admissions arrangements have an influence on segregation.

Taking into account school number and type, the use of catchment areas – and, to a lesser extent, distance criteria – is associated with higher levels of segregation. This is primarily because they lock in existing patterns of residential segregation; however in some cases catchment areas in particular have exacerbated segregation by encouraging a mutually determining connection between school quality and house prices. A number of studies have reported a house price premium in areas with better or more popular schools.

At the same time there is some evidence to suggest that segregation has been reduced overall in areas where choice has been most effective (although choice has also worked to polarise schools by intake in those cases where it has been skewed towards specific families). In short, there is reason to believe that a system of extended choice in the UK may be preferable from the perspective of integration to a system in which places are allocated by catchment areas, and perhaps also distance criteria.

With regard to the nature of local schools, selective, fee-paying, voluntary-aided and grant-maintained schools are all associated with higher levels of segregation. An unanswered question here is whether these results are driven by diversity or selection, as these schools all have in common that they can recruit widely against schools with narrow catchment areas. In addition a number of studies have reported some association between specialist schools and increased segregation. These are early results, and again the relative contributions of diversity and selection are unclear; however we should be aware that the issue of segregation under choice is linked importantly to these supply side issues.

Conclusion

The system of school choice in the UK does not have some of the key characteristics associated with efficiency and equity benefits. In particular, supply side constraints are severe. This appears to be allowing for covert selection by popular schools. If school choice in the UK is to deliver greater benefits than is currently the case, real contestability between schools needs to exist. This is likely to involve significant expansion of capacity, characterised by a lack of selection, either in the form of new state schools or of a new non fee-paying independent sector, along the lines of charter schools in the US. The evidence suggests that the latter would be more effective. However, very little work has been conducted on the overall cost-benefit analysis of introducing such new forms of contestability into school systems. This would be a prerequisite of any developments in this area.

Patient Choice: what are the policy implications?

Introduction

Out of the patient choice policies reviewed here, only the UK choice pilots report substantial take-up of choice by patients: the international evidence has invariably reported low take-up. The internal market GP fundholding experiment had a similar experience. For this reason we dedicate some time to the issue of take-up for patient choice policies and support for patients making choices.

Low take-up of choice

There is no simple explanation as to why low take-up has so often been the case. It would be unreasonable simply to rule out the possibility that patients have often been satisfied with local provision: a substantial proportion of patients have exercised new choices in order to attend a nearer provider. On the other hand it seems unlikely that this is the full explanation: for many of the international policies, choice has been attached to waiting time initiatives; and although these have been shorter than the six month UK choice pilots, they have nevertheless have been long enough for us sensibly to assume that the whole explanation does not lie with a natural preference for local provision.

Choice policies internationally have generally been accompanied by vague and variable arrangements for funding following the patient. In most cases funding has landed at the level of the municipality rather than with the provider. Providers have therefore had little financial incentive to accept or encourage new patients. Funding does not yet follow the patients for the majority of UK choice pilots; however when

choice is introduced nationally, individual Trusts will gain and
lose at the full tariff. Part of the explanation may therefore be
that, with the exception of the UK choice pilots, providers have
had little financial incentive to facilitate patient choice. This
seems the most likely explanation.

One issue worth noting is that, both internationally and in
the GP fundholding experiment, take-up of choice by patients
has been low where choice has been offered to them through
a GP. This suggests that the issue of supporting patients in
choosing may not be best resolved simply by relying on GPs
as agents of choice. This result is particularly important in the
context of the GP fundholding experiment, as GP fundholders
were able to contract with providers on a case-by-case, and
by-results, basis. In their case the explanation for (apparently)
low levels of patient choice is not that providers had little
incentive to accept their patients – the evidence is that they
responded to this incentive; rather, GP fundholders did switch
patients between different trusts but had little incentive to
facilitate patients' preferences in doing so.

There are various possible explanations for why this might
have been the case: it may have to do with paternalism or
intransigence on fundholders' part; survey evidence is conflicting
in that whilst fundholders said they were enthusiastic about
offering patients choice, few actually consulted with their
patients when making those choices on their behalf.
Furthermore, their patients remained indifferent to the issue;
finally, there is some evidence to suggest that fundholders'
incentives as contractors may have got in the way of their
incentives as agents of patient choice. Whatever the precise
cause, the result is itself important because, when choice is
introduced nationally at the point of GP referral, GPs and PCTs
will play an important role as the agents of patients' choices.
For those who see a value in patients themselves making choices,
then, the proper role of the GP as agent of choice needs to be
addressed. The research teams studying the LPCP have already
acknowledged this issue as a potential obstacle when the LPCP
is rolled out nationally: their survey results, unlike those carried
out during the fundholder pilot, indicate that GPs are less than
enthused by the prospect of having to consult with their
patients regarding their referral decisions, creating a real risk

201 The College of Health undertook work to assess the role of PCAs in the choice pilots and suggested that further experimentation is needed to develop models of support, and to assess the additional support that patients at risk of social exclusion might need. It noted the advantages of having clinically trained PCAs who can provide condition-specific advice to patients as well as non-clinically trained PCAs who can advise patients across a range of different health conditions. Coulter et al found that patient satisfaction was equally high with the PCAs both in the CHD (where PCAs were clinically trained) and in the London Patient Choice Project (where they were not).

of GP obstruction to patient choice. The ways in which GPs might be sanctioned or incentivised to cooperate with the scheme, and other possible means to overcome this potential obstacle, will be examined further as part of our forthcoming research programme on choice and primary care.

High take-up of choice

It is reasonable to assume that the PCAs have contributed substantially to high take-up for the UK patient choice pilots. Survey evidence suggested that they were popular with patients; in addition patients more favourable about their PCA were more likely to express satisfaction about their experience of choice and, importantly, were more likely to take up choice in the first place (the usual methodological caveats associated with retrospective survey evidence of course apply). The question for PCAs is not whether or not they have been effective in general; rather the question is which elements of the package have been particularly important and for which patients[201].

This question will prove important as subsidies for support currently arranged by PCAs – for example transport – will not be universally available when choice is introduced nationally. Assuming the package of support offered by PCAs as it currently exists is not fully sustainable, it is therefore important to understand how it might be targeted. Our on-going research into support for patient choice will address these questions.

Efficiency benefits

The form in which the PCA package might be sustained will depend to a large extent on any efficiency benefits associated with choice. Policy for choice in the NHS has been perhaps the most advanced in ensuring that incentives are effective and fall at the appropriate administrative level: when choice is rolled out nationally trusts will gain and lose at the full tariff with each patient. In addition there is no indication that providers have been ill equipped in terms of administrative and budgetary freedom to respond to choice. The issue is therefore not the introduction of incentives but the effects they will have and how they might be adjusted.

The evidence on the systemic outcomes of patient choice

(which is fullest for the UK) is encouraging in some respects, but uninformative in others. The aspect that is encouraging is that, for those benefits that have been monitored there is evidence that the threat of exit has worked to improve the quality of provision. Benefits have been distributed in the way in which advocates of choice would predict; that is, both non-choosers and choosers have benefited from patient choice. In this respect it would appear that the theory behind the policy is correct, and this is crucially important.

On the other hand the evidence is limited because – unsurprisingly – it does not provide a very complete picture of the overall systemic outcome of choice: the worry that choice will distort priorities and discourage co-operation between providers has not been shown to be right, but it has not been shown to be wrong either. Neither is it yet clear whether any efficiency gains associated with choice and payment by results according to a fixed tariff will outweigh the associated costs in terms of introduction, support for patients and planning. In short, the evidence so far is *in line with* its advocates' general predictions, especially on the important question of how the instrumental benefits of choice might be distributed, while not being conclusive on a cost-benefit analysis.

Selection of patients

A further general criticism of choice policies is that they extend both the means and the motive for providers to select patients. Policy can address both the means (through restrictions) and the motive (through incentives). The most interesting evidence on the issue of selection is from the internal market. There was in fact no evidence of selection by trusts. However there is some evidence on a lack of selection by GP fundholders which found that fundholders did not go in for cream-skimming, *despite the incentive to do so*. It seems that a combination of a crude stop-loss insurance scheme, limited costs for fundholding procedures and natural motivation to help their patients (and perhaps a lack of necessary information) came together to prevent cream-skimming.

This is a local result, but is encouraging in showing that, in practice, cream-skimming might be prevented without total and perfect risk-adjustment. The point is to make sure of what works in practice and then adjust regulation and incentives accordingly: for example by locating admissions procedures elsewhere, or by adjusting the tariff that follows patients around the system.

Conclusion

Britain is ahead of many of its international contemporaries in the introduction of choice. While choice schemes have existed for longer in countries such as Denmark and Sweden, choice schemes were introduced there without some of the important elements needed to produce efficiency gains without compromising equity. For example, a lack of information about the options open to patients had a clear impact on take-up. Denmark's experience has led them to move step by step closer to a model of choice characterised by real contestability – information for patients, financial incentives for providers to take on new patients and the ability of providers to increase capacity. The lesson for the UK here is that the introduction of choice schemes which do not have all the key criteria are unlikely to be successful.

Because the UK is ahead of many other countries in introducing choice, there is little clear evidence from the research on long-term impacts. However, there is evidence from the UK that choice in healthcare can bring real efficiency gains. For example, the threat of exit was used successfully by GP fundholders to lever improvements in secondary care. In this case, choice operated as a lever for both productive and allocative efficiency. This should give us confidence to proceed in extending choice in the UK. Take-up of choice is likely to helped considerably by a PCA package, as offered in pilot schemes. However it is not yet clear which elements were most helpful, and more should be done on this before the programme is rolled out.

SMF programme of work on choice and voice

Consultation on findings from the evidence base

Following the seminar on 23rd September 2004 which the Social Market Foundation is holding to discuss these findings, we will send this paper out to consultees in Government, Parliament, Whitehall and academia for comment. A final draft will then be printed and published in October. All readers are invited to supply their comments to the authors, Ann Rossiter at arossiter@smf.co.uk and Jonathan Williams at jwilliams@smf.co.uk.

Issue for SMF programme

1. Choice of provider

This review of the evidence has thrown up some critical issues for consideration in the extension of choice in public services. In particular, there are elements of scheme design which must be present to at least some degree if the introduction of contestable choice is to be beneficial in terms of both efficiency and equity.

There are three criteria which are all required if efficiency gains are to be made:

1. freedom for service users to choose a provider

2. adequate demand sensitivity, including the possibility that supply can expand with demand and sufficient financial and managerial discretion for services to be able to respond to choice

3. funding follows the service user to an appropriate administrative level: e.g. to the direct service provider

There are a number of other, more minor considerations, including ensuring that providers do not have conflicting objectives, such as to reduce costs while facilitating user choice.

In addition, there are a number of associated criteria which, if the above criteria are met, are required to be present if efficiency gains are not to be at the cost of equity:

1. preventing service providers from actively selecting users

2. sufficient capacity at system level to ensure that limited supply does not create a situation in which good providers are able to select users covertly. It is clear that, in some cases, this will require new forms of provision

3. a systemic or governmental response to failing providers. This might include active support, management change or closure

4. the freedom to choose being made meaningful for all users through information and support, including the provision of objective performance data, advice, assistance with access costs (travel etc.)

This list of policy design criteria does not present us with a checklist by which we can judge whether an individual choice policy should be adopted or not. Extending choice in the UK will necessarily involve the adaption of existing services with all that that entails, including needing to take account of the current views and behaviour of both professionals and service users. The SMF will use this list of factors as a starting point for research into the extension of provider choice in key areas of public services.

2. Choice, voice and personalisation

There is a lack of clarity about the relationship between choice in its different forms and other user involvement ideas in the debate in the UK. This is particularly true of 'voice', but is also true of 'personalisation'. As mentioned earlier in this paper, there is also a lack of clarity about the meaning of these terms. An important element of our work going forward will be the attempt to define these concepts and to explore the interrelation between them. In doing so, we start from the following position:

1. Voice and personalisation can be understood either in terms of outcomes (recipients having an effective say, having a personalised service) or as policies (use of questionnaires and surveys, representative boards, and so on). As outcomes, whether or not they are compatible with, or furthered by, choice is strictly an empirical question.

2. Choice and other personalisation policies can be mutually reinforcing: giving recipients a choice of service and/or provider, and giving them a service designed to fit more closely their needs both serves to improve allocative efficiency and drives up satisfaction with public services.

3. Choice and voice policies are not necessarily alternatives to each other. Rather they can drive services to meet the same goals. However proponents of choice often regard voice mechanisms as having failed to produce public services that are responsive to user needs, and therefore as an option to be discarded when introducing or extending choice. On the other hand, those with concerns about choice systems have tended to regard voice mechanisms as a panacea for creating more responsive public services, and to regard choice mechanisms as their antithesis. An expression of this is the concern that giving service users a choice of providers reduces us to the role of consumers[202] by suggesting that if we do not like the service that we receive from provider A, we simply move to provider B. Both these views are an overly simplistic analysis of the dynamics of choice and voice in public services.

Choice theory is based on the premise that competition for users will cause service providers to improve the services on offer. The ability of service users to choose a provider means that the service provided will more accurately reflect their needs. However, this dynamic does not depend on a mass outflow of service users leaving provider A for provider B. A small number of the totality of service users leaving provider A for provider B is likely to provide a signal for provider A to (a) examine the level of service it is providing and (b) to improve the quality of its service and/or tailor the service more closely to the needs of users.

202 This is one of the main arguments of Citizen-consumers, *New Labour's marketplace democracy* Catherine Needham, Catalyst Working Paper 2003

203 Hirschman, A: *Exit, Voice and Loyalty: Responses to Decline in Firms, Organizations and States*. Harvard University Press, 1972

In order for provider A to understand why service users are abandoning it in favour of provider B, it will need to engage with service users. In other words, it will need to employ voice mechanisms to reach this understanding. The more effective the voice mechanisms used by provider A, the less likely it is to suffer an outflow of service users in the first place. In other words, it is in the interests of provider A to pay close attention to the needs of service users and to its comparative performance because of the potential threat that service users might exit in favour of provider B.

In other words, it is the threat of exit rather than exit[203] itself that should generate the incentives to service providers to closely meet the needs of its users. The more effective the voice mechanisms used by a provider, the more likely that provider is to closely meet the needs of service users, and the less likely the provider is to lose users and income.

SMF research programme

School choice

One major issue thrown up by the evidence on choice is that the system of school choice in the UK does not meet the criteria highlighted above for a choice system which will generate efficiency and equity benefits. Most significantly, supply side constraints are very severe. Also, little support is available to parents in making choices. Our research will look at the mechanisms available for removing these capacity constraints and their practicability and cost-effectiveness. We will look at increased capacity within the state sector, the scope for the development of an independent no-fee, no-selection sector to compete with the state sector, and the management of failing schools within the state sector. We will also look at the need and scope for supporting choice. In this, and in all other areas of policy we will consider, we will also look at the potential for the exercise of voice mechanisms to reinforce the exercise of choice.

Choice in primary care

The introduction of choice policies in primary care raises a number of difficult issues. The first – PCT commissioning – is fundamental to choice in general within the NHS and is an example of the exercise of collective choice. Patients will make choices in consultation with their GP, but they will also travel down the pathways set out for them by PCT commissioning. The experience from the internal market, however, is that commissioning at a level higher than the GP can do much to *restrict* patient choice. We will examine how to maximise the responsiveness of PCT commissioning to the needs of patient, including looking at how personalisation of services can be introduced, and the role of voice in reinforcing responsiveness.

It seems likely that the government will seek to provide patients with increased choice of GP as well as increased choice in secondary care. However, the model of contestability found in GP fundholding, where GPs purchased services for their patients but also (in theory at least) competed for patients and surpluses themselves does not appear to be favoured. In so far as contestability is desired to make primary care providers effective (both as providers and as agents of patient choice) a number of issues need to be addressed when choice of GP becomes a reality. This includes capacity within the system, the ability of patients to make an effective choice and what support will be available to those choosing. We will consider how these reforms might be introduced in order to increase the responsiveness of GPs to individuals needs.

Social housing

The evidence base considered in this paper did not extend to housing policy. However, for those in social housing, choice is very limited. We will conduct a short review of the national and international evidence on the operation of choice in housing policy, and look at policy options for increasing choice for social housing tenants in the UK.

Timetable and programme of work

We will be setting up an Advisory Panel to oversee the SMF's programme of work on choice, voice and personalisation.

We will be hosting a number of seminars on these issues over the remainder of 2004 and the first half of 2005. We aim to report findings on choice and primary care, and school choice by spring 2005, and to produce a report on social housing in the summer of 2005.